The Arms of God

Cross of the Sisters of St. Mary of Namur
(Photo courtesy of Sister Margaret Young, SSMN)

The Arms of God

The Sisters of St. Mary of Namur, Western Province

Sherrie Reynolds

WIPF & STOCK · Eugene, Oregon

THE ARMS OF GOD
The Sisters of St. Mary of Namur, Western Province

Copyright © 2011 Sherrie Reynolds. All rights reserved. Except for brief quotations in critical publications or reviews, no part of this book may be reproduced in any manner without prior written permission from the publisher. Write: Permissions, Wipf and Stock Publishers, 199 W. 8th Ave., Suite 3, Eugene, OR 97401.

Wipf & Stock
An Imprint of Wipf and Stock Publishers
199 W. 8th Ave., Suite 3
Eugene, OR 97401

www.wipfandstock.com

ISBN 13: 978-1-61097-117-1

Manufactured in the U.S.A.

Contents

Preface / vii

Acknowledgments / ix

Chapter 1. Giving Their Lives to God / 1

Chapter 2. Every Child in a Catholic School / 25

Chapter 3. Global Citizens, Missionary Sisters / 48

Chapter 4. Free Will Was God's Idea, Not Mine / 83

Chapter 5. Radical Openness to the Future / 107

Bibliography / 129

Preface

UNDERNEATH AN armless crucifix in the airport in Brussels is a small plaque with the inscription "You are the only arms I have." The Sisters of St. Mary of Namur (SSMN) have been the arms of God in schools, hospitals, prisons, and parishes since their founding in Belgium in 1819. They were founded to meet a need in Belgium, then came to the United States to meet a need, and have since gone to Rwanda, the Democratic Republic of Congo, Mexico, Brazil, Britain, Canada, Cameroon, and the Dominican Republic because there was a need. They have built schools to meet a need and then left the schools in the hands of others when they believed that the need could be filled by them. They have worked with children, adults, youth in gangs, and people in foreign lands, always with a preference for working with the poor.

The Sisters of St. Mary of Namur, like many other consecrated religious, have lived through a period of extraordinary change following the Second Vatican Council in the early 1960s. When asked about the purpose of the Council, "the Pope simply walked to a window and flung it open. The purpose of the Council, in a word, was *aggiornamento*—bringing up-to-date. The Council would open the windows of the Church and let in fresh air."[1] The Council changed the liturgical and sacramental experiences of all Catholics, but it changed the lives of religious communities even more dramatically. The Sisters of St. Mary lived through these changes in a distinct way reflecting their history and heritage. My

---

1. Corinna Laughlin, "The Second Vatican Council."

Preface

initial interest in interviewing the SSMN was curiosity about the lived experiences of this change.

As I became better acquainted with them, I found a group of women who are better educated than most women of their generations and more widely traveled than most Americans. They are good-hearted people who have, as many of them said, "given their lives to God." They see their work as ministry, for which some are paid and some are not. They are talented and creative with a deep love for music, art, literature, and dance. Some of them have had difficulties, including serious medical problems. The "retired" sisters, some in their eighties, are still working in a variety of ministries. Some of them are still traveling to help establish foundations in Africa and other countries. Theirs is an uncommon view of retirement because they are an uncommon group of women.

This book has evolved from my observations and conversations with the sisters as well as interviews with many of them. As I talked with the sisters, I began to believe that young people like the students I teach, especially the women students, should know about them. In many ways, this book is for these young women. I am acutely aware of the limitations of my attempt to translate a presence into words on paper. I have done it as faithfully as I know how. I make no claim to having written an objective story. In my experience and that of many others who have spoken to me about the sisters, it is impossible to be around these women and maintain any pretense of objectivity. Their love and their joy draw us in, and we are irrevocably changed for the better for having met them.

The first chapter describes the transition from young lay woman to a Sister of St. Mary. Stories of teaching are in chapter 2. Stories of missionaries are presented in chapter 3. Vatican II and its aftermath are the focus of chapter 4. The future of religious life in the Sisters of St. Mary of Namur, including new forms of religious life, ends the book.

Acknowledgments

I AM grateful to the sisters who shared their stories with me and to Sister Cecille, Sister St. John, Dorothy L. Gray, and Clarice Peninger, who gave freely of their time and talent to edit this book. I am also grateful to Diane Murray, who listened to every word of the many versions of the chapters and was untiringly encouraging, and to Sarah Boukhari and Freyca Calderon for all of their help in preparing the manuscript.

Chapter 1

Giving Their Lives to God

WHY DID these seventeen- and eighteen-year-old women decide to become Sisters of St. Mary, consecrated to a celibate life of service? Many of the sisters spoke about a sense of being called to religious life, which they described as a "tug" or a "pull." Each had a sense of being called, and many mentioned that they felt it was what they were supposed to do or were meant to do. Some welcomed it; however, several of the sisters talked about resisting the call for a period of time. In some cases they did not feel worthy or thought that they were not holy enough or that there was an obstacle to their being accepted.

When they talked about their initial reasons for becoming a sister, most sisters said they wanted to "give my life to God," "make God the center of my life," "do something for God," or "be close to God." Others talked about wanting to "do good," to "do something with my life," "to contribute to the good of the world," and "to work with the poor." Sister St. John said that St. Thomas Aquinas had a passionate desire for God and that he wanted to unify all his desires into one. She said, "So that's what it is all about, whether I am cleaning the stairs at Our Lady of Victory Convent (OLV) or teaching somebody in the prison. It's that desire to bring in the kingdom and to be for God." Most of the sisters said that they were drawn to the Sisters of St. Mary because of sisters they knew or because they wanted to work with the poor. Some sisters felt drawn to the Eucharist.

DRAWN TO THE SISTERS OF ST. MARY

A common reason the sisters gave for entering was that they felt drawn to the Sisters of St. Mary whom they knew. Most of them knew these sisters either because there were Sisters of St. Mary in their family or the sisters taught at their school or they were friends of their parents. Some of them talked about the "mystique" of the sisters and "knowing them from a distance." Like most young Catholic girls, they were curious about what the sisters did and how they lived. One sister said, "It was my first experience with sisters. They had a long habit, and I wondered all the normal things—like do they ever go the bathroom and when did they ever eat." Another sister commented, "They had on long habits, and they walked so nicely that I thought maybe they were on roller skates."

But when the sisters talked with the young women about vocations, they did not present an unrealistic picture of their lives. One sister said, "It was about sixth grade that I first got the inkling that I might want to be a sister. I think it was because Sister Roseanne used to talk to us about the life of a sister. What struck me was that it wasn't just all the positive stuff. She let us know that there were hard times, too, that you didn't always get to do what you wanted to do, and that sometimes it was really hard."

The sisters spoke fondly of their relationship with the Sisters of St. Mary. Most of them talked in some way about the joy and caring that they saw in the sisters. One sister said, "I grew up across from the Sisters of St. Mary. I lived in a typical little neighborhood. They had a white frame house and were just as much a part of the neighborhood as we were. I was always running after them. We would play in the school yard, and we would see the sisters, and everybody would charge them and walk with them wherever they were going."

Another sister said,

> I knew the sisters when I was growing up, and I went to high school to a different set of sisters who were stiff and impersonal. I always wanted to be a sister from the time I was six. During high school my best friend and her mother and I were talking about my best friend entering, and the mother asked me, "Which order are you going to enter?" I said, "The Sisters of St. Mary. I would never enter [the order of sisters who taught her in high school]. They are so inhuman and so stiff." The mother said, "Maybe God wants you to go and loosen them up." That scared me. It got me thinking, why do I want the Sisters of St. Mary? I think it was their joy. I always saw them as very simple and very joyful. After I entered, when they said the motto was about simplicity and joy, I thought, "I saw that in them." I don't think I really had an idea about what religious life was about. There was a lot of hero worship of several sisters that helped me grow up and helped me decide, I think. I finally made the decision. I went back to my best friend's mother and said, "All right! It is going to be the Sisters of St. Mary."

Sister Devota first knew she wanted to be a sister when her aunt, a sister, visited.

> I was about three, and Mother told us that Sister was coming to visit. I asked her, "Why does she dress like that?" She replied, "Sister wanted to give her whole life to God, and they dress in that uniform so that they don't have to worry about changing dresses and styles and all." What struck me, and I can still feel it, was that she gave her whole life to God. In my heart I said, "I want to give my whole life to God." When she came, she was a very tall, well-built person. When she was standing at a chest of drawers talking to my mother, she was so tall that her arm was on the top of that chest of drawers. I remember looking from the bottom of that big black dress right on up to the top of her veil, and I said to myself, "She gave her whole life to God?" I wanted to do that. . . . When I entered the convent, I didn't care if I scrubbed floors the rest of my life; all I wanted to do was to give my life to God, and that has stayed with me. I would do this for nobody else, and only for God would I have given up a husband and children.

THE ARMS OF GOD

Sister Martin Joseph said,

> The Sisters of St. Mary were always a part of my life. In fact, I've often said that I knew when I was three years old that I wanted to be a nun. We were living in a big apartment—well, it was big to me. I was only three years old. I was sitting on the curb. Our Lady of Good Counsel [OLGC], run by the Sisters of St. Mary, was right across the street. There was a big expanse of grass, and there was the church, Blessed Sacrament Church. I'd watch the sisters go over with the students. Mother came out one day and asked me, "What are you thinking?" I said, "I'm going to be one of those sisters over there." I knew sisters because of my aunt [who was a Sister of Saint Mary]. I never lost the feeling that I wasn't going to get married and I wasn't going to have kids. I loved people, but I just knew that I loved God. I had a sense of God from the very beginning. I never lost it.

DRAWN TO THE POOR

Some young women were drawn by the sense of service and especially the way the sisters worked with the poor. A sister recalled,

> When I was in high school, we started a group that would go to a poor area in Fort Worth. We used to go down and teach catechism once a week with the sisters. I was always struck by the fact that we could leave but the kids stayed in that situation—broken families and poverty and violence and gangs. I think I've always had a feeling for the poor, the less privileged.
>
> So I did that throughout high school, and at the same time I was dating someone I really liked, and I didn't know what I was going to do, so I decided after graduation I would go to college for a year. I told this plan to God. I decided that if I hadn't met anybody that I thought I wanted to marry or [discovered] something else I wanted to be after that first year of college, then it was a sign I was supposed to enter the order of the Sisters of St. Mary. I knew I somehow wanted to work with the poor. The Peace Corps was beginning, and the whole question of even social work and all that was all something that you didn't just jump in and do as a young woman my age,

at least not in that day and time, at least not in the milieu I was being raised in.

I went to college for a year. A little after Christmastime, I went and spent a weekend at the novitiate, which was at the University of Dallas [UD]. There were vibrant young sisters there, and I mostly decided I wanted to enter. I entered because I wanted to work with the poor.

Sister Miriam was drawn to the Sisters of St. Mary because of their sense of service, concern about the poor, and the way they encouraged the students to think for themselves. She said that her parents had a sense of service and caring about other people. "Many times my dad would bring somebody home who was down and out. He would say to my mom, 'Honey, could we put Joe up for tonight, and get him something?' My mom would say, 'Sure.' I saw my parents do that over and over again." Sister said that she appreciated the respect the sisters showed each individual and, in high school, the way the sisters helped her to learn to think and develop a sense of herself as an individual. She also appreciated the sisters' international experiences. She said,

> Even though I thought of them as being kind of behind the walls, I thought, "These women know what is going on in the world; they care about what's going on in the world."
>
> Then, of course, in high school we were encouraged to do service projects. In those days it was really visiting the nursing home or going over to Grant Street [a poor area of Fort Worth]. I saw the sisters involved in things. Sister Margaret was over at Grant Street working with juveniles and a lot of difficult situations. Somebody else was at the nursing homes . . . , but the sisters went with us. I watched their interaction with people, and their interaction with people was just so wholesome, joyful, and authentic. For me, that was very much a part of why I think I was drawn to think about joining the sisters.

Even with all these things that Sister Miriam appreciated about the sisters, she did not intend to join when she finished high school. In fact, she said that even though the thought of joining was occurring to her from time to time, she tried not to think about it. She didn't want to make the senior high school retreat, and she did not say the line in the Stations of the Cross that says, "Grant that I may love you always, Lord, and then do with me what you will." She said, "I would not say that last line because I had this feeling that God wanted me to do something that I didn't want to do. But of course, obviously, I remembered it. I just didn't say it out loud."

During Sister Miriam's senior year, one of her good friends in high school said that she was going to talk with the superior about entering and asked Miriam to go along. She decided to go, just to "see what it was like and see what she'll say." A week later, Miriam received an application in the mail, but her friend did not. She said that the superior must have mixed up their names, but, nevertheless, she kept the application.

She said, "The fact that I had this application in my bottom drawer kept haunting me. So I pulled it out one day and looked at it again. It had some things in there about having to purchase clothes, and I didn't have any money at that time. I had told one of my friends that maybe I was considering this, but I'd probably have to wait a while until I could get a job and get some money. She told her aunt, who was an assistant at an oil company downtown and was one of those women who supported charities. One day, I opened up the mail, and she had sent me a check for a hundred dollars. I thought, 'What's happening? What's happening here?' After that I thought, 'Maybe this is what God wants me to do.'"

Sometimes events and circumstances confirmed a sister's sense of vocation and of God's providence. One sister had been planning to go to the Benedictines. She went to confession to talk with the priest about it, and she waited at the church for over an hour, but none of the priests came. After a while she decided that they were not coming and went downtown to visit a friend. She said, "While I was there, [another friend] came in. She said, 'You're just the person I want to see. I have a scholarship to go to Our Lady of Victory College, but I don't want to go. I'm going to get married. I thought maybe you would like to have it.' I said, 'Yes, I think I would.' I said to myself, 'I guess that's it; God is calling me to something else.'"

Some sisters wrestled with their vocation before and after entering. Some made a commitment and did not look back. Some went through a period of discernment and then either left the congregation or made a renewed commitment to stay. One young woman believed that she had a vocation but wasn't sure. She asked a priest, "If you have a calling for a vocation, but if you didn't want to do that—you wanted to get married and have children—but you felt somehow that God was calling you, does that mean you do or do not have a vocation?" The priest said, "If you feel like you want to do something else, probably that is what you are meant to do." "I remember leaving that room so free because I wanted to get married and have kids. I thought, 'That's it. That other feeling that I had wasn't anything I had to listen to.' The next day was the end of the retreat . . . I can still see him [the priest] walking up—he was very patriarchal. He said, 'Last night I had a dream, and in the dream a little bird came to me, and she told me this story. I think I gave you the wrong information.' He told the exact story I had told him, and he said, 'If a person feels God's call, one has to stop and listen to that, even if you don't deep inside feel inclined to want to do that.'"

Some sisters came from deeply religious Catholic families but not all. Some families were less religious, and several came from families of mixed religious background. Sister Mary Frances found her Catholic family "inconvenient."

> We were the only Catholics growing up in the town. When I was nine years old—that was a very happy year of my life—I was madly in love with Tommy. We were in the fourth grade. I said to my sister, "I'm going to marry him." She said, "Well, you know you can't because we're Catholic and he's a Baptist." That destroyed my life. I was so dumb. . . . I don't know why I believed her, but being a Catholic was kind of like an albatross, and I was not really pleased about being a Catholic. In

the town there were Methodists, Christians, and Baptists, and my friends were all one or the other, and going to church on holy days of obligation was a strange thing to do. Growing up, we'd put pickles on our hotdog buns so people didn't know we didn't eat meat on Friday. We went to catechism at St. Cecilia's every Sunday morning—eight o'clock mass, catechism lesson after that, memorization of catechism in the afternoon—all of this was just such an interruption in my life, which was social and musical. I would go to communion on Sundays, and these dear Sisters of St. Mary would be there faithfully after teaching school all week long. I never was impressed by anything in the Baltimore Catechism, but something of the joy of the trinity of sisters who cared about each other and cared enough about God to come and do that resonated with something in me that I was not even aware of at the time.

When I was getting ready to go to college my senior year, I said to my father, "I guess I'm going to a Catholic college because I need to meet Catholics since I'm Catholic." My father was not real happy about it, but I got a scholarship and went to OLV for my first year of college. Something happened during that first year. I made a silent retreat. It was the first three days of silence I had ever spent in my life. I was very touched by the silence. The nuns, as well as the college girls, were in retreat. The whole place was in silence.

Throughout that year at OLV, my freshman year of college, I went to mass every morning. I didn't like to get up early, but there was something about being there, going to mass, and going to communion. Something felt at home about it.

In the spring, I decided, "I think I won't go here next year. I think I'll go to a school where there are boys." I had never been to an all-girls school before, and I had never gone to a Catholic school before. That was the only year of my life that I did, but there was still this thing. I felt like I was feeling something going on inside of me, but I didn't exactly want it. But I knew there was something pulling me. At Thanksgiving, I talked with Sister Mary Ellen when I was home. I said to her, "I think I'm going to be a nun." I didn't know anything about a vocation or even what it meant to be a nun exactly. I just felt like I was being pulled. My friends couldn't understand what I was doing. My father said, "Are you unhappy?" My grandfather said, "I'll send you to any college you'd like to go to if you just won't do this right now." But it was strong enough, and there was no logic about it, no process of discernment; it was just something inside of me that told me, "This is what you are supposed to do."

PARENTS

Some parents were supportive of their daughter's decision to enter the Sisters of St. Mary, but many were not. One sister explained, "Neither of my parents wanted me to enter. Over the years I've come to figure that out. I think your parents know how happy you can be in married life, but they don't have any clue how happy you can be in religious life." Sister Ann Vincent said that her mother "cried and cried" when she told her that she wanted to enter the Sisters of St. Mary.

Some parents were reluctant because the young woman was their only child. Others felt that she had not seen enough of life to make that decision. Still others were taken by surprise. They just had not thought about their daughter as having a vocation since the daughter had not talked about it. One said, "I entered the community because I felt that God was calling me to something else than what I was living. I wasn't quite sure what it was. I had some friends who said to me, 'I think you're being called to religious life,' but there was no history in my family, and I had really not too much inclination until this happened when I was a senior. So then I batted it back and forth and finally made the decision in the late summer to go ahead. My dad found it very difficult that I was going to do this because I had never thought of it. I didn't realize how difficult it was for them, but they didn't say I couldn't do it, and so I did enter."

Another sister said, "I was supposed to enter, but my mom thought that I should see more of the world before entering the convent. So my oldest brother and my mom and my sister and I drove up to Washington, DC, and New York. My brother was smart. I was to be back home just four or five days before I was due to enter the convent. So I wasn't going to have very much time to think about it. We were in Detroit on our way home when we got the message that my father had suddenly died. On my way home, I told my brother that obviously God didn't want me to enter the convent right now." She said that her brother drove her to OLV to tell the sisters that she wasn't coming. Her brother waited in the car while she went in to talk with Sister. As she was leaving, she said, "I'll be here Sunday." When she told her brother, he said that he knew that was what she was going to do. "Well," she said, "I didn't." Her dad really didn't want her to enter. He asked her to promise to leave the convent if she was not happy. She said that those were his last words to her. Then, she added softly, "That has been a challenge."

Some of the sisters waited to enter because of family obligations. Sister Cecile was one who had to wait. She said,

> In high school, I was inspired by the joy and simplicity of my teachers. I knew I wanted to offer my life to God as they had done. My mother had taught me that vocation is a gift to be prayed for, not presumed. After a senior retreat at OLV in Fort Worth, I told the Jesuit retreat master of my desire. As my father's work situation was unsteady at the time, the priest advised me to stay home and work. Three years later, when my father was assured of engagements all year, I was free to follow my dream. From the day I visited Mother Benita at Our Lady of Victory to ask permission to enter until the present day, I have never doubted that this is where I belong. Five of us entered the same year, one of whom had to leave for family obligations. By the grace of God, our group of four was still intact sixty-two years later, until 2005 when God called Mary Elizabeth home.

Another sister had wanted to be a sister most of her life, but her mother was a single parent with a daughter who had health challenges. She told her mother that she couldn't enter because she felt that she was needed at home. Her mother said, "You're dating such and such a person. He's from Chicago, and he's in the army. You could get married and go to Chicago. I wouldn't interfere. The other girls are going to get married. I wouldn't interfere at all, and [the child] is my responsibility."

She didn't enter right away, however, because her aunt, a Sister of St. Mary, intervened. She said, "No, you're not going to—not now. I don't want you to have to wait twenty-five years to get your BA degree. I had to wait that long. If you're in love with a man and he is in the army, you'll wait for him, won't you, and you'll get married. Now, if you have a vocation, get your education first, and then you can enter and you won't have to work on your degree for twenty-five years. If you love Him now, you'll love Him two years from now." She finished two years of college and then entered.

Sister Mary M. wanted to enter, and she wanted to teach. Her immediate family was fine with it, but some of her Protestant relatives asked a lot of questions. She said that one of them told her that she could teach without entering, but she replied that she wanted to do both. She said that she had a relationship with God, but "after I entered, I discovered so much more about developing the relationship with God."

Some mothers were very supportive of the decision because they had felt drawn to a vocation at a time in their lives. One sister said that when she begged to make the retreat at OLV, her mother said that she had often wanted to make a retreat there to find out what her real vocation was but could not because she had to help with her siblings. Her mother agreed that the young thirteen-year-old could go, but when she asked the sisters, she was told, "You can't keep silent for three days." Not only did she stay quiet during the retreat, she said, "I cried that afternoon when we left. I knew that's where I wanted to spend the rest of my life."

ENTERING

Once a young woman decided that she wanted to enter, she had to fill out an application and submit a letter from her pastor. Some didn't realize they had to ask. Sister Teresa said, "It never occurred to me I had to ask permission to enter." After she wrote her letter, she mentioned it to her parents. They were happy about it. After she had made her final vows, her parents told her that they had always prayed that one of their children would either be a sister or a priest.

Another sister said, "I came to get measured and all that. A date was set for September 8. That was very important . . . to have a date; otherwise, I might have just gone on, and the eighth was the day no matter what. It was difficult. I would say leaving home was the hardest thing I've ever done. Some people get excited about leaving home and entering, and to some extent there was an adventure and excitement and, of course, a challenge, but I really did miss the environment of my farm and all, but I have learned much. I gained more than I left, for sure." Another sister who had a difficult time said, "My mom was my only parent, and leaving her just about killed me dead. I was so homesick for her I thought I was going to die. It was really, really tough."

THE HABIT

By the 1950s the habit was beginning to be modified in stages. First, they stopped wearing the coiffe and guimpe. One sister remarked, "Some of the very judgmental eighteen-year-olds thought it was terrible because we could see their necks! We were kids, and we thought nuns should be very austere and suffer." One of the sisters who wore it, on the other hand, commented that they "no longer wore the hot and unattractive coiffe and guimpe. What a relief!" In the 1960s the sisters had the option of wearing a modified habit [the one that looks like a skirt and blouse with a veil] and finally to the current practice of wearing clothing of their choice with a cross [the cross pictured on the front cover of this book] that distinguishes them as Sisters of St. Mary.[1] Sisters still dress in

---

1. Sister Margaret Young, e-mail message to author, October 23, 2010.

Giving Their Lives to God

a variety of these styles, choosing the one that is most comfortable for them or most consistent with their beliefs.

One of the sisters is a very attractive woman who, today, dresses beautifully and with an artistic flair. She found the clothing she would wear as a postulant challenging, especially the shoes, which they had had to purchase and bring when they entered. She said, "Oh, but buying the postulant shoes . . . I went all dressed up . . . into the shoe store, and this nice young man says, 'May I help you?' I said, 'No, thank you.' I couldn't buy those old granny shoes that day, but once I was here, that was the fashion. That's what everybody wore, so that was fine."

Sister Mary F. found an interesting solution to the shoe problem. She went shoe shopping in Boston. She bought one pair of "nunny" shoes and then asked the salesclerk to bring some more comfortable black shoes for other occasions. Finally, she asked if he could dye the white part of some black-and-white saddle oxfords. She reported that he said, "I've never heard of a nun wearing shoes like that." She replied, "All they said was black." She bought the shoes but did not notice that the soles were red. She said that years later she found out that when she was a novice and postulant, the sisters referred to her as "the one with the red soles" because when they knelt for communion, the red soles of her shoes were distinctive among the black soles of the other novices and postulants.

The sisters entered as postulants. After about six months, they took the habit and a white veil as a novice. They were in the novitiate for about two years, one of which was the "canonical year." That was a year when the young woman studied religion but otherwise neither studied nor taught. Following the novitiate, the sister took the black veil and made vows of poverty, chastity, and obedience. For the first three years, they made vows for one year at a time. Then, they made vows for three years. After a period of time that varied at different times in history, the sisters made "final" or "perpetual" vows.

Some of the sisters entered at a time when they had to sew the habits. One of them said that making the habit was the most sewing she ever had to do. There was a lot of detailed work. One sister described the habit that she wore when she entered in 1940 as a simple habit that tied in the back. It had big cuffs with buttons on them and a little ruffled French cap that tied behind. Another sister said that when her mother brought her to the college the first night and saw those postulants, she remarked, "It's really snazzy; they've got French maids here."

The aprons of their habits had quarter-inch pleats that were sown all the way across the apron. They would make the pleat and stitch it, then go down about an inch, stitch it again, go down about an inch, stitch it again, and continue that way down the front of the apron so that it would hold its shape. They would then launder it and iron it very precisely. Over time, dust would get in the pleats, so every few months they had to undo the stitching to launder inside of them, restitch the pleats, and launder it again. As the pleats got worn, they would remove the stitches from the pleat and make a pleat next to where the old one had been.

Novices wore the same habit as the sisters: a long, black, tightly fitted dress made of wool serge, which is heavy wool. The veil was white and precisely starched. Everything had to be very white and starched. Everything was noticed, and it had to be done in a precise way. The habit was hot, especially in Texas summers with no air conditioning. When asked if they were hot in the habit, one sister replied, "Well, maybe we were hot, but we weren't any hotter than anybody else was." Other sisters told a different story. One said, "The sisters had to be asked to clean where they had been sitting in chapel because the nuns would be perspiring so heavily and leaving wet spots where they were sitting."

Sister Ann Vincent said that there was a sweet-smelling vine growing on the pergola, and when they were on the way in for a recital, Sister Marie Celine told them to take a piece of it in with them and hold it. Sister said, "We didn't change our habits after working all day, and I'm sure we didn't smell like a petunia."

The sisters wore the habit for all occasions, including recreation. Sister Mary Patricia took the young teenaged sisters over to the elementary school to play volleyball at night, and then they would go in for night prayer. Sister Dorothy said, "We would go in just dripping, little puddles just all over, and the clown-eyed rings from the sweat over our eyebrows."

THE NOVITIATE

The earliest novitiate was in New York. Sister Mary Alberta was the only one of the sisters I interviewed who said that she attended that novitiate. She said that when she was in the novitiate, there were six or eight women there and that most of the other novices were from Ireland and one or two were from Canada. Sister Mary Michael said that her aunts, Sister Margarita and Sister Mary Vincentia, were the first novices in Texas and were sent to New York for their novitiate.

Most of the sisters I interviewed went to novitiate at Our Lady of Victory, and some of them were sent to Belgium for part or most of their novitiate. In 1960 the province opened a novitiate at the University of Dallas. It was closed in 1968, and novices were sent to New York again.

The sisters talked about the fun they had in the novitiate. Their demeanor changed when they talked about it, and they seemed lighthearted even when describing hard work and chafing under rules that sometimes seemed too restrictive. One sister described her novitiate experience as follows: "From the beginning I felt very welcome in the congregation. Life was very structured; every minute of the day was scheduled with prayer, work, study, and recreation. I remember the novitiate days as filled with laughter and fellowship, as well as challenges."

LAUGHTER AND FELLOWSHIP

Like most situations where there are older and younger women, the older ones played tricks on the younger ones. One sister remembered a time when the novices told the postulants that they were supposed to take off their caps and put them down the laundry chute. The novices put their caps down there and waited for clean ones to show up. When they figured out that no clean ones had arrived, they went down the five or six flights of stairs to find their caps. Since the laundry chute hadn't been used in years, the recovered caps were covered in dust. They shook the dust off the best they could and hoped nobody noticed.

Sister Ann Vincent recalled when she was new that Sister Francesca, who was rather short, did the high work, while Sister Francesca gave her, although much taller, the low work such as cleaning the baseboards. Another time Sister Francesca asked Sister Ann Vincent to wash the commodes on her first or second day as a postulant. She said that she "went right to it." She added that it wasn't anything new to her because she did that at home. The novice mistress noticed and told Sister Francesca, "You don't do that the first day!" When Sister Francesca told Sister Ann Vincent, she said, "That's okay. I've done it before, and I know how."

Sister Mary Fulbright laughed as she recalled a trick her friends played on her. "Three of my very best friends came to college here that same year, so I was going to college classes with them. We had a rule of silence. We couldn't talk to them. One Monday, I was in chapel, and the college students were in front of us. Postulants were in about the third row, and the college students were a couple of rows in front of us. Three of my friends walked in and sat in the pew in front of me. They had gone over to visit my mother, and the three of them had on my clothes!"

Sister Ann Vincent grew up in Nebraska. She had never seen a magnolia tree until she saw the one in the grotto area by the convent. She pulled a branch down to look at the blossom, and the branch broke off. That was during the time that they had to make a public confession if they damaged or broke anything. Sister said, "We kept that quiet, but they made me suffer through it all. In music one day, we were doing Gregorian chants with Sister Alice Claire, and one of the responses that we did had 'magnolia' in it. When we'd practice that, they would nudge me, or they would clear their throats. It was just misery."

The sisters had public reading, where one person would read and the others would do mending. Sister Rita Claire, who was known for "liking bugs and any kind of animal or anything," had a horny toad in her sewing basket. Sister Ann Vincent said, "Sister Marie Celine, the novice mistress, was petrified of anything like that. We knew Rita Claire had this horny toad, and it was going to get out anytime. You know how much reading we heard."

Sister Ann Vincent talked about the bonding in the novitiate. She said, "We were always together, and we were called the big five. We just felt for each other, and I think we were all very simple people, and our lives, our backgrounds were just like that. Our families were just very simple, average, middle class. There was just a mutual relationship. There was something we each had that we gave to each other."

Another sister said, "We bonded quickly in the novitiate, and that was a plus to have a group. There were four of us, and later a fifth came. There was a lot of support like that. We all went through the same things." Sister St. John said, "There was something very beautiful about it. It was trying to learn who God is for you, and it was developing wonderful friendships." As she described these friendships, Sister St. John is sitting in the parlor of a room where she eats meals with women she has known for all of her sixty-three years of religious life. She mentioned a conversation at lunch today between herself and a sister who was in the novitiate with her. These are not only deep and wonderful friendships, but they are also long-lasting ones. She said that none of them expected that "extra gift that came" with religious life. Speaking of her life today at the retirement center with these sisters, she said, "We did the dishes together in the novitiate, and we're still doing the dishes together."

RULES AND STRUCTURE

The structure and "rules" were challenging to some and less challenging to others. Sisters who tried to explain this suggested that it either depended on the kind of structure they had experienced at home, or on their personality, or on the style of the novice mistress. One sister said, "We had a lot of crazy rules. While nobody really recognized it as being controlling, there were controls. The greatest control you can have on people is control of money. And you weren't supposed to go to sleep at night if you had a penny in your possession. What you read was controlled. It was a very controlled environment." Sister Mary F. had difficulty with the rule of silence which, for these sisters, meant that they only spoke at mealtimes. Sister said, "This rule of silence didn't make any sense to me, so I went to Sister Marie Celine, and I said, 'I don't think that rule makes any sense. I don't even think it's charitable. You know, in Waco we would speak to a stranger on the street, and here I can't even talk to the sisters who taught me.'"

Sister Mary F. had brothers who went to Texas A&M University, and Sister Marie Celine knew that they had been in the corps (ROTC). The corps had very strict and crazy rules, especially for the freshmen. Sister Mary F. said,

> I had entertained the novices with some of these stories, so when I told Sister Marie Celine I thought the rule of silence was not charitable, she told me to look upon some of these rules like some of those rules they had down at A&M for the Aggies, for the freshmen. She didn't try to make it holy; she didn't baptize it. It was just simply a part of learning to be a sister, and that's what I needed to do. I guess she recognized this maverick in me and that I would have come right back at her if she had tried to baptize it. But I didn't have any answer for that; it satisfied me. So my novitiate days, while we were

required to do those ridiculous things, she helped me to develop an attitude toward things that has gotten me through a lot.

Another sister reported that she "had a little trouble with the discipline." She said, "During the 1940s and 1950s, we led a very strict life." She mentioned the "silence, few clothes—all habits—hard, hard work." They had to ask permission to "write letters, phone, or get personal necessities." They "never visited any home nor ate in public." Another sister said, "We had to get permission for everything." Others said that they "communicated among themselves without a word. We laughed, but not out loud."

The young sisters were expected to be ladies and were taught proper ways to conduct themselves. They were Texans and Sister Dorothy said, "In some cases they had this terrible Texas accent." In the novitiate, Sister Marie Therese gave us diction classes. It was to teach us how to be ladies. It obviously didn't take too well."

Another sister said, "We started some college classes at the University of Dallas. We would drive over there a couple of days a week, but it wasn't totally school; there was a lot of learning scriptures, learning about history of religious life; it was a very positive experience—learning in that big old building upstairs and downstairs and all the basements and outside what you could do, what you couldn't do, all these rules and regulations, weaving in and out of that. In some senses, it was not at all a restricted environment as I recall it."

Another of the sisters said the novitiate "was very, very structured, and I thought that it was rather strict because I didn't come from a strict background. We were very free at home, we kids. Our parents were not strict. My dad was very kind and loving, and he didn't talk much. I found it very strange that we would get fussed at for things we didn't even mean to do, like break something. But that is how it is and that is how they had to train us, I guess. But I did keep quiet. I didn't ever voice my opinion on things. I had them inside of me, but I would never voice them, even when I was a younger sister. I guess it took years before I could do that."

One sister said that the novices weren't told to plant vegetables upside down or any of the things they had read about in *Lives of the Saints*. They were just told things like "Go clean the dormitory." She told a story from those dormitory-cleaning days. The way that they cleaned the outside of the windows was to sit in the open window, hold on with one hand, and clean the window with the other. One day, the novices were cleaning windows on the fifth floor, and the sister in charge had told them not to clean the windows on the outside if they were afraid to. Sister said that she figured that if a novice was afraid to clean the windows on the outside, it meant she wasn't sure of herself. She said, "Show offs like me were happy to do it." So she cleaned the outside of the windows. One day, the screen broke. She was holding it with both hands, having forgotten to use one hand to hold on, and she began to fall. She said, "I was yelling for someone to come get this screen before I dropped five stories and broke it. It didn't occur to me that I might drop *me* five stories."

Sister Mary Patricia was cited by several sisters as a very sensible novice mistress and later Sister Dorothy said,

> I loved my novitiate, unlike some people who did not have a happy one. I had a glorious one. Sister Mary Patricia would say, "Here, here is twenty dollars, go plan a party." Sister Alice Claire, who followed her, said, "Dear, go buy white yellow napkins and blue plates and white cups." Mary Patricia treated you like you had some sense, I guess, and some maturity and responsibility, whereas, poor Sister Alice Claire, we were awful to her. She said, "Stand up"; we sat down. If she said sit down, we stood up. It was so bad that a couple of us went to Sister Mary Patricia and said, "It is absolute rebellion." I don't know why they didn't send us home, honestly. We were just typical, ornery seventeen- and eighteen-year-old kids. I think that some bought the party line, as I did for many years. Like at nine o'clock, it was grand silence, and Jesus could have appeared, and you would not talk to him. I did my best to follow

all that, and I remember later hearing Sister Mary Patricia say, "Oh dear, I didn't pay any attention to that. I thought if I had something to say, it was only charitable to say it." I never in those days gave myself permission to think like that. I think that was the big difference. A whole bunch of us tried to be the good sister, and I would project that that is the difference between Sister Mary Patricia and Sister Alice Claire. Alice Claire had an image of what the novice director looked like and how she should act, whereas Mary Patricia said, "Dear, just do what you think best."

NOVITIATES IN BELGIUM, TEXAS, AND NEW YORK

After World War II, some of the novices were sent to Belgium to the novitiate. Some had difficulty with the language (French), but all of them were grateful for the international experience. The experience of living in Belgium was broadening, especially since some of the sisters were there when the first novices began arriving from Africa. One of the sisters who was chosen to go experienced a dilemma because she did not think she had a vocation. She asked herself, "What am I going to do? I've lied to the sisters; I don't intend to stay, and yet I don't want to give up a trip to Europe." She went to confession to "this wonderful old confessor. . . . He was a missionary and had been all over the world, and he spoke English, so I went at the end and told him . . . that I had lied to the sisters and I felt really terrible about it. He said, 'My precious child, why don't you calm down and let God work in your life?' And so, every week I'd go talk to him. Well, it was a wonderful vocation that I experienced; you know, I'd go to that chapel; they had a beautiful stained glass window of the crucifix, and I would just go and pray and ask Jesus to guide me. I did get a vocation." Sister Josephine is still a sister.

Many of the sisters reported that they had trouble with the language in Belgium. Everything, of course, was in French, and those who did not speak French or did not pick it up quickly, essentially had no speaking relationship with the other novices or the novice mistress. That aspect of it was very difficult, but most enjoyed getting to know the roots of the order and its spirit. One sister said,

> There were difficulties due to the language, but at that time Mother Elizabeth was the superior general. If there was a reason she could send me to England for a week or two, she did. That kind of helped. There was a young Belgian sister who spoke fluent English, so Mother Elizabeth would send her down to the novitiate just to spend an hour with me, just so I could speak English. There were other English-speaking novices, but at that time we had the rule of silence. We had thirty minutes together in the evening only, and my French was so bad that finally our novice mistress said that no one could speak English because I wasn't learning French. That was very difficult. We were sitting around, unable to communicate.

In the 1960s, the novitiate moved from O.L.V. to the House of Study at U.D. One of the first sisters to go to U.D. as a postulant called it "the beginning of a new era." She said, "Vatican II was just starting in 1962. The first year, we studied French and Philosophy, Metaphysics, and Philosophy of Man.

The novitiate at U.D. was closed in 1968. One sister said,

> I was going to enter August 22. Sister Alice Claire was the mother superior. Two weeks before, I got a call from her, and she asked if I wouldn't mind going to the Buffalo novitiate because they had decided they were going to close the novitiate here. They didn't tell me the reason, but I wanted to enter, so I said, "Yes." Two weeks later, I entered on a Sunday morning at UD at the House of Study. And at four in the morning, we got up to catch the seven o'clock bus to downtown Dallas. I had only been out of Texas maybe twice with my family, so Buffalo was like going to the end of the earth the day after I entered. Of course, in those days you didn't question it. I mean, if it were in this day and age, you know, you would have questioned things and wondered differently. There was not going to be a novitiate group here, so since I was the only one who was actually entering that year, I had to go to Buffalo.

Giving Their Lives to God

PROFESSED SISTER

When the sisters made their vows, they traded their white veil for a black one and were referred to as "professed sisters." In the early days, all of the sisters were teachers. They attended school during their novitiate for two years at OLV and taught while they finished their degrees in the summer. One sister who taught for a year before making her vows had a challenging year. She said, "I don't know how you get anybody who doesn't plan to make vows to go back in a classroom."

The sisters received their new assignment each year on August 15. They came to the motherhouse for retreat with their steamer trunks packed for moving. They did not know where they were going until the list was read at a meal following the retreat. Newly professed sisters made their vows at ten o'clock in the morning, heard the list read at the noon meal, and were ready to leave immediately following. There were no opportunities to go back and say goodbye to people at the previous assignment. This seemed difficult to me. I asked one of the sisters who had described herself as a little bit spirited and rebellious as a novice how she went from a rebellious novice to the sister who can accept that this is "just the way it is." She said, "A certain amount of rebellion wasn't strong enough to overcome what I came for. I came to give my life to God, and there were no *ifs*, *ands*, or *buts* about it, and I had the impression God had wanted me to come. If he wanted me to go, he was going to have to show me. And he didn't." With that commitment as a guiding principle, she said that she just dealt with everything else as it came along. She said she thought married people were more like that then, too. "You didn't think you could arrange your universe to suit yourself. There were other people in it. There were situations in which your initiative might have been challenged but not destructively so and not by the people I most admired."

In the late 1950s the sisters began junior professed training for younger sisters who were as a group referred to as the "juniorate."

The junior sisters were at the University of Dallas where they lived and attended classes. One sister reported, "The juniorate years for me were really my blossoming years. I came back here after I made vows, and Sister St. John was the juniorate mistress. I loved the House of Study. The whole atmosphere was so good. It was so good to get in touch with the person forming me. She was such a big influence in my life and in my growth.

Chapter 2

Every Child in a Catholic School

Curriculum studies scholar Patrick Slattery said that public schools were largely considered "nondenominational Protestantism . . . with readings from the King James Bible and Protestant rituals."[1] Slattery reports that the Catholic minority reacted by establishing a parochial school system that expanded dramatically from the 1840s to the 1960s, reaching a peak of more than twelve thousand schools and seven million students in 1965. Parents were strongly admonished against sending their children to public schools. Several sisters reported that the theme of the period was "every Catholic child in a Catholic school." As a result, Catholic schools were bursting at the seams (one sister had sixty-five first graders), and young sisters became teachers with very little preparation.

THROWN INTO TEACHING

Many sisters reported being "thrown into" teaching. The young sisters taught right out of the novitiate and then earned their credentials in Saturday and summer classes on what several of them called "the twenty-year plan." They became reasonably good

1. Slattery, *Curriculum Development*, 74.

teachers in a short time, in part because older, more experienced sisters mentored them. Sister Ann Vincent said, "I worked with Sister Pauline in knowing how to teach a class and what to teach. She was just like a guardian angel to me and very helpful. But as I grow older, I look back at this incident or that situation, and I wonder how I did it." Another sister said, "I learned that if you do impossible things or at least make a stab at them, it really does something to you."

Sister Mary Jean's first teaching position was as a replacement for "a very well-known and well-liked sister named Sister Maureen." She thought, "Here I am, coming in out of school and having never taught. . . . I remember praying that kids wouldn't leave or that parents wouldn't take their kids out when they saw me." Sister Mary Jean had fifty-four students in her first grade class that year.

Sister Frances said, "I was in the novitiate, and our novice mistress came to me and said, 'Today you're going to need to teach Sister Marie Therese's class. She's sick and can't go to class.' [It was as if] she was saying, 'There's nobody there to do the dishes, so you're going to have to go and take care of them the best you can.'"

Sister Frances's first day of teaching was memorable. By the end of the day, she said, "I was sick. I went to Sister Marie Celine, and I said, 'I feel [sick]. I don't think I can go to rosary this afternoon at five. Could I just go to bed?' Then, I began to think about the day. We didn't raise the windows, and by noon it got warm and overheated. Everybody was kind of uneasy because we didn't have fresh air in there. I thought that was a lesson I would ordinarily know about, but this was my first day. I didn't look at windows; I looked at pupils."

Sister Louise said that she had been teaching piano when Sister Marie Celine "called me to her room after night prayers and said, 'Don't bother preparing your government class for tomorrow. You're going to start teaching third and fourth grade.'" Sister Louise added,

Fortunately, your older sisters would watch over you; and if you were struggling with something, you always knew that you could go to any of them and ask for help, and they would do it, and they would do it graciously. We had a sister who was the supervisor of schools, and she would drop in on your classes, see how you were doing, and offer advice. If you were really struggling and she could see that you were, she would probably put a word into the ear of somebody who could help you, and you'd find yourself being guided along. No matter what you wanted or what you wanted to know, she would stop anything she was doing, and she would try to do it for you.

One of Sister Mary F.'s mentors, Sister Mary Ellen, "was one of the founders of the University of Dallas. She was my first superior. She was just a great teacher. My first day of teaching we had the kids lined up outside, and we were coming in. She kind of got in step with me as I was leading my class in. She said, 'Sister, the best thing about today is that you will never ever have to live it again.'"

Sometimes mentors helped by reminding the young sisters of their gifts. Sister St. John was working with Sister Agnes in the library after school when some of the girls in the sister's class walked by and gave her a big greeting. She said that Sister Agnes said, "Your children love you." Sister St. John replied, "And I love them, but I feel like I can't give them what they need." Sister Agnes said, "Your children have had experienced teachers, and they will have them again. Right now, give them what you have—youth and enthusiasm and devotion." St. John emphasized: "That's the kind of philosophy we had. That's why we had good students—because that tradition was passed from one to the next."

Some sisters did not want to teach, but they wanted to be a Sister of Saint Mary, and so they became teachers. Some of them struggled with teaching, while others enjoyed it right from the beginning. Sister Ginny wanted to teach since she was young. "I've always really loved little children. I would line up my dolls around the kitchen table and teach them when I was little. I had classes and kept a grade book and everything. I just loved teaching." Sister

Dorothy also loved teaching. She said, "I took to it like a duck to water. I loved it. I really did."

Even the sisters who became marvelous teachers later did not always take to teaching immediately. Sister Rita Claire had no intention of becoming a teacher and had not prepared for teaching. She said, "The provincial called me in one day; it was near the end of the novitiate training, and she said, 'Sister Mary Ellen would like you to continue as her assistant taking care of the books.' I'd be visiting all these different convents and looking at their bookkeeping and helping them with their books. 'Or,' she said, 'you could teach.' All during the novitiate, the other young sisters in the group had some practice teaching with Sister Mary Bridget, who was our educational supervisor, but I didn't have any. I thought, 'What is God asking here? Am I to be a bookkeeper?' And I thought, 'That is not enough contact with people. I want to know families, and I want to help people.' I didn't want to be a teacher. [I wondered], 'What is God saying?' And I said, 'I think that God is asking me to be a teacher.' So I told [the provincial] that I thought I wanted to be a teacher, but I said, 'I haven't had any teacher training or anything.' She said, 'We'll take care of that; Sister Mary Bridget will help you.'"

Sister Rita Claire said that she went into her classroom for the first time with no preparation whatsoever. She said, "My mentor had not done any lesson plans with me or anything. I think we taught religion first, and I got through that in about ten minutes. Then, we had reading, so I went down the row, and each one of them read a little something, and they read well. The first teacher had been a good teacher. By recess I was finished with everything. I thought, 'Well, I'll start over.' About that time Sister Mary Bridget appeared at the door and was listening to me teach. I went to the door, and I said, 'We're finished.'" After that first day, Sister Mary Bridget began helping her each day after school.

Sister Mary Frances was thrown into teaching when, after her second year of novitiate, she was told she needed to take organ lessons. "In those days they didn't tell us what they had in mind—just 'you need to take organ lessons.'" She found out later that she was going to teach all the singing and play the organ because the pastor had fired the director of the choir. Then, she was asked to teach second grade because she was small. She said that Sister Agnes, who was in charge of the education of the young sisters, decided "small people would be good primary teachers."

STRUGGLES

It is not surprising that these young sisters had some difficult times as teachers. With their characteristic humor and lightheartedness, the sisters reported on some of these times. Sister Dorothy said that when Sister Teresa was the superior, she came to visit each classroom. When Sister Teresa visited her room for the first time, Sister Teresa said, "I have come to hear the children." Sister Dorothy said, "What class would you like to hear?" She replied, "Reading would be nice." Sister Dorothy said, "I gave her the book, and I left. I went over to the teachers' lounge. I read and had a grand time. In thirty minutes, when reading period was over, I went back, and I said, 'How did they do?' She said, 'They were very good.' I said, 'Good. Thank you. Come again.' I had no idea that she was coming to see me. She said she had come to hear the kids."

After making first vows, Sister Dorothy replaced Sister Rita Claire, this time in the seventh grade. Sister Rita Claire had been a science major. Sister Dorothy said,

> I walked in, and she had all of these mobiles in different configurations of atoms. My first thought was, "Oh, I am over my head here." But the night before, Sunday night, she called me, and she said, "We had better go over the lesson plans." She sat down, and she said, "We are on the subjunctive case in English." I said, "I don't know what that is." "Well, they need a review," she said, "so we can go to verbs." I said, "I don't know grammar at all." It got worse and worse and worse, so by the time the evening was over, I was in tears, and it ended up [that the principal], Sister Mary Frances, would teach my seventh

grade English, and I would teach her eighth-grade religion because I [had] only learned English grammar when I learned Spanish; I just missed it, somehow, totally.

"I can remember sitting in that classroom, and the kids would come up to the desk, and I would say, "Sit down; you are out of your seat without permission." Then they would sit down, and one would raise her hand, and I would ignore it because I knew I didn't know the answer. I was awful as far as having any sense . . . thank God they were good. It was fun, but I don't know how they learned anything.

One sister said that there were workbooks that had reading in the front and phonics in the back so that you could have a reading and phonics lesson with the same story in the book. She said that one of the young sisters assigned to teach did not understand the intent and just went straight through the book. So the first semester, they had reading, and the second semester they had phonics. Nobody told her.

At the age of nineteen, Sister St. John was sent to teach fifth and sixth grade. She had trouble teaching and didn't have any discipline. "I took one look at the children, and they took one look at me, and we both knew who was in charge, and it wasn't me." She said, "I loved the kids, but I wasn't sure that I could go on with teaching. But I came up with this idea that I was really called to religious life, so there were no *ifs* about it. . . . It was just a question of you accept life the way it is. You are not here to evaluate; you're here to work for the Lord."

Sister St. John said, "I'll never forget the first day we did standardized tests. Like most young teachers, I was going too fast. As soon as *I* knew it, I thought the kids did. We corrected our own tests in those days. I had several students who were outstanding and did beautiful work and, of course, I had them on top of the stack. I said to Teresa, 'Look how well Robert and Alex and Rosemary did.' She said, 'Those are the ones who would have learned if you had never been born. Now, show me the ones you taught.'"

At her next school, she had trouble with discipline, as she had earlier in her career. The principal had told her to direct her students to do a certain thing in the procession, and they didn't do what she told them. "I told her, 'They didn't do what I told them.' She said, 'You're a woman, aren't you? They are children, aren't they? Tell them what to do and expect them to do it.'" She noted, "The principal did not say, 'You're the boss. You are an adult. You are a woman, and they should expect you to show them what to do.'" Sister St. John said that changed her teaching. She said that it gave her a sense of who she was. She had been thinking of herself as this young person who didn't know too much; and from that time on, she thought of herself as a teacher.

Sister St. John said, "I loved books; I loved learning, but I said to Sister Genevieve, who was my senior teacher, 'Don't you get tired of teaching the same books all the time?' And she said, 'You don't teach books. You teach children.' And that is the way it is. The books are just kind of the channel."

Sister St. John talked about how much she liked seventh and eighth graders. She said, "They're my favorite group." She paused a moment and then said, "Of course, my favorite is whomever I'm working with at the time." One year she taught at Cistercian Prep School in the morning and at the University of Dallas in the afternoon. Of the prep school, she said, "You know, you really have to put out all your energy to hold those guys in line. Then I went up to UD, and they're sitting taking notes. It's down at the grade school that they tell you who you really are." Somebody asked her how she could teach elementary school in the morning and university in the afternoon. Sister St. John told her, "You teach who's in front of you."

This reluctant teacher, who persisted in teaching only because it was part of her gift of herself to God, clearly has become a teacher. When she was in charge of transitioning the sisters from their old building to the new center, which was certainly a full-time job, she said, "But of course, I had to teach." So she taught as a volunteer in a senior citizens' program at a community college. She doesn't seem to care if it is teaching children in elementary school, university students, seminarians, sisters in the "junior ranks," or people incarcerated by the prison system. It truly does not matter to her because she says: "It is always about the people." Sister St. John was given the opportunity to study for her doctorate. She turned it down because she said, "I didn't want to be a scholar; I wanted to be a teacher. By this time, I'd learned how, and once you learn how, you hold onto it."

GOOD TIMES

The sisters enjoyed teaching in other parts of the country, especially in California, which was part of the province. Sister Mary Alberta talked about California as if she were describing a different world. She had never seen an avocado or an artichoke before she went there. She said that there were so many students from other countries that it was like teaching at the United Nations.

Sister Mary Jean was sent to California to help an older teacher who had forty-five students in her class. She said,

> I loved it out there because we had a sister, Sister Theresa, who was superior out there, and she made it her business to see that we saw everything, from Disneyland to the sequoias, Kings Canyon, Yosemite, San Francisco—all of those places. This was a whole new experience for me. We just hadn't done anything like that. When school started, I had twelve kids registered. When I knew I had twelve kids, I knew what was going to happen. In those days everyone had large classes. They were not going to leave a young sister like that. One day in October we were at recreation, and the telephone rang. Theresa went out and answered it, and then she came back, and I said, "Every time the phone rings, I get so scared." She said, "Why?" I said, "I am afraid they are calling me home to Texas." She said, "Why is that?" I said, "Because I only have twelve kids." She said, "Well, I haven't told them yet." I thought that was so wonderful. I spent the whole year there.

One of the reasons the sisters were good teachers in spite of their lack of preparation may be because they were such learners themselves. They talked about some of the moments when they learned from the children. When she was principal and teacher, Sister St. John noticed that one group of children had performed very poorly on the standardized test. When a priest came in and said he wanted to teach, she asked him to teach her eighth grade so that she could take the group of students who had performed so poorly on the test. One of the things she discovered was that no one had ever read to them.

> There were three kids who were absolutely illiterate. They were Mexican, and one kid said, "When I start to learn here, we go back there. When I start to learn there, we come back here."
>
> [O]ne of those three . . . was a fragile little lad, a white-skinned, freckled, blue-eyed Mexican. He couldn't learn to read. I knew there was some psychological factor, but I couldn't figure out what it was. It came time for the school picnic. He was the first to bring back his mother's signature that he could go with somebody else and she wouldn't hold him or her liable. He wasn't at school the day before the picnic. He walked a couple of miles to tell me that he wouldn't be at school the next day. I said, "What's the problem?" He said, "We've got problems at home." I said, "Tell me about it." He said "My dad beat up my mom last night, and now he is in jail, and she is in bed, and there's no one to take care of the new baby." [The woman had just given birth.] I said, "Do you have any food at home?" He said, "We've got milk for the baby and the rest of us are big enough." [Big enough] to go hungry is what he meant. So we put some food in the car and went over to his house, and it was as he had said.

Sister St. John said, "I could tell you stories about those children forever. It's the stories you remember. The math and English are important, and you work hard at it, but that is not what changes souls. It's the relationships."

Sister Mary F. told about an exchange in class that was particularly meaningful to her.

Those kids had insights, and their questions taught me so much. I told the kids (this was a seventh- and eighth-grade class) that if they asked me a question that I couldn't answer, they would get extra credit. One day a kid raised his hand and said he had a question. He said, "We studied and you said that God is all powerful and that God loves us just so, so much. If God is all powerful and loves us so much, why does God allow us to do evil?" I said to that boy (I can still see him standing there by his desk), "You get a point. I've not gotten a satisfactory answer to that question. I think it's one of the most important questions in human society." But I was a good teacher, so I didn't just rely on me; I threw it back to the kids. I said, "Does anybody have an idea?" Another boy put up his hand and he said, "In the book of Genesis, we studied that God made man in his image and likeness. God is totally free, so if we are to be more like God, we have to be free, and that means we have to be free to do wrong." I said, "That's a pretty good answer. That makes sense to me." But then the part I love, the first boy jumps up and says, "I've got it! The one thing God wants from us is our love, and to love somebody you've got to be free."

That's what this kid was getting to—[the one] who said the one thing God wants from you is your love. Nobody can give that but you, in your own unique, special way. I think that we, in justice, we as Sisters of St. Mary have to be respectful and responsive to our sisters who believe, in faith, that this is the way that I must do things because it's the way we were taught to do things. I think we have to be respectful of that because we taught them that. We're responsible for that attitude, that belief. We can't just say, "No, that's wrong," and drop them. You can't do that. It's not the way God would have us to be. I think there are a lot of rules that make it extremely hard for sisters to respond to God in that unique, special way. I think we're making major strides in that. And again our Sister Mary Patricia was so much [a part of] that. Whatever you were doing, she might disagree with it, but she always let you realize it was okay. That has been the root of my theology ever since. It puts a different picture on everything.

A PREFERENCE FOR THE POOR

The Sisters of St. Mary, then and now, have a preference for the poor, and many of the schools in which they taught were in very poor areas of town. Sister Frances taught in one of those poor schools, built by a pastor of a small parish. She said, "It was a poor parish, but [the pastor] decided the important thing was to have a school in the parish and have all of the children in the parish come to the school. After the school was built, he got a big Packard, an old one, and he went around and he gathered up the children. It was like Santa Claus's sled stuffed with dolls in the back. After he had delivered the children, then he came by and got the teachers."

Sister Mary F. also taught and was principal of a school in a very poor area. She said, "When I got up there, the school was dirty, and it was just awful. It was the first time I'd ever been there. It was just a small school, about a hundred and twenty kids. [They were] very, very poor. I had never been principal, but when I walked into that school, I went home and I said, 'I've got to write the superintendent and ask for permission to put off the opening of school until October because we've got to clean this place up. We cannot have those children come to school here.' So we did that. Their parents were wonderful, wonderful people. They just didn't have any money."

Sister decided to have school uniforms. She helped the students get the uniforms. Then she said, "One of the hardest things I ever did, but I think I would do it again—it was hard—we'd have uniform inspection. We'd tell the kids, 'After school you've got to take those uniforms off when you play, so they will be clean.' And they did that. They'd go home and change clothes and come back and everything was fine."

It was common in the Catholic schools of that time to combine grades, so that first and second were together, third and fourth were together, fifth and sixth were together, and seventh and eighth were together. Sister Mary F. had the problem that it was August, and she only had three teachers. She found a teacher, but did not have the money to pay him. She went to the superior, Sister Mary Patricia, and told her,

> "There's a guy who would be willing to teach, but he can't teach for nothing." Sister Mary Patricia said, "How much would he have to have?" I said, "He would have to have two hundred dollars a month." She said, "Hire him." I knew we didn't have any money, but she said, "Hire him." I hired him, and we paid him. Divine intervention? No, it wasn't divine intervention; it was people, and this is a very important part of my theology. I don't think God intervenes in human affairs. I think human beings either do that which is pleasing and makes life more the way God would have the family of God be or we don't. So the people were the interveners that paid for that.

Some of Sister Mary F's tasks were even more difficult. She said,

> One experience taught me the church was wrong. At that time, if you married out of the church, you were excommunicated. One of my former students had eloped and gotten married. Pastor came over to the school one day and told me that this young man had been killed in a wreck. He said to me, "You know I can't have the funeral. I think it would be easier if you told his mother than if I went over." Boy! So I'm going over to tell his mother that he's been killed. I can't think about that without crying. I sat there and I said to her, "You know and I know Father cannot have the funeral. But you know and I know that your son is with God." I simply couldn't look her in the eyes and believe that God would do what the church said. The church was wrong. I guess that experience, perhaps more strongly than any other, gave me a frame of reference that when the church speaks, I don't necessarily say "yes." And when the church is speaking today, I'm saying "no" to several things. A lot of that goes back, though, to this kid who was killed.

Sister St. John pointed out that their preference for the poor also meant that they did not earn very much money. She said, "The struggle is always not just to be where people can afford you. When we started out, we earned $270 a year, so we didn't save much for our retirement." She added, "People have always been good to us." Other sisters commented about that as well. They said that there were physicians who took care of them and hospitals that made sure that they received care. One said, "People brought in groceries, and they still do." Clearly these kindnesses, while helpful, cannot provide for the needs of the retired sisters completely. The church does not provide for them, and the smaller numbers of sisters entering religious life coupled with the aging of the congregation puts the financial future of the sisters in jeopardy.

INTEGRATION

The Sisters of St. Mary integrated their schools before other Fort Worth schools were integrated. Sister Jane said that it followed from their awareness of the poor since it definitely was harder for black people in this city to make a living than it was for white people. Sister Jane said that the sisters integrated their schools before it was mandated and before the public schools integrated their schools. She said, "It was the era of the civil rights movement. By the time I entered the community, we had been one of the first to integrate. It didn't always work out. There was a lot of fear and animosity here in Fort Worth. Fear mainly [that] if you go to school with students, you're going to marry them; that was the ultimate conclusion instantly. We lost a lot of students. Parents really were afraid for their younger students. There was a lot of price to pay, but the sisters went right ahead."

Sister St. John said that when they first integrated the elementary school, they got some ugly telephone calls from parents. One parent said that she was going to take her child out of Catholic school and she would probably go to hell and that would be the sisters' fault. Sister St. John said that if the mother made that decision, it would not be the fault of the sisters.

Many of the sisters talked about the joy of teaching in schools that are, as one sister said, "characteristic of what the whole St.

Mary's spirit was; it was multicultural, multieconomic, and multiethnic. It's always been that way. To me it's a microcosm of the kingdom, and I love that."

COLLEGE ON THE TWENTY-YEAR PLAN

The sisters were undoubtedly among the best-educated women of their generation. Most of them hold master's degrees and some earned PhDs. All of them have attended a variety of institutes and seminars in the United States and in other parts of the world. As novices, they taught during the academic year and took classes in the summers. By the time they completed their teaching certificates, they had taught for several years. Several sisters credited Mother Eleanor with making sure that the sisters finished their education. One sister said, "I think our Mother Eleanor was a great educator. She was the one who told me to go to school. She made special efforts and succeeded in having our sisters go to colleges and universities. She wanted our sisters to be as well educated as we could possibly manage. The sisters started going out to universities and learning. When they came back, they had new ideas. It was sad in a way because Mother Eleanor was personally responsible for that, and she had the hardest time coping with it."

One sister talked about the older sisters who went to college: "I mean, they were over 65, but they studied and learned and went to college. To see these old religious women walking across the stage to get their college diploma was a real feat. Most of them succeeded. They had those years of experience behind them from teaching, but to have to sit down at that stage and study college-level material!"

Sister St. John recalled one summer when she and Sister Cecile had been sent to college at the West Coast branch of Catholic University. She said to Sister Cecile, "Here we are, at two o'clock in the afternoon, sitting under a shade tree reading poetry, and that's what we're *supposed* to be doing?"

PRINCIPALS AND SUPERINTENDENTS

Sisters became administrators in much the same way as they became teachers: they were given the job and then, often years later, they attended university classes and earned their administrator's certificate or advanced degree. They almost always continued to teach while they were principals, and they seldom had any clerical help. Most of the time, it worked out. Sometimes it didn't. One sister said, "After my fourth year out of the novitiate, I was made principal. I was twenty-six or twenty-eight years old. I remember the maintenance person. He knew everything that went on with the sisters inside and out, and he said, 'Well, they sure scraped the bottom of the barrel this year.' The man wasn't even educated, and he knew how green I was."

One of the sisters had a very difficult time as principal. She said, "At the end of [that] year, Mother Devota asked me to be principal of a high school. I became the principal, and I didn't know anything about being principal. It was a very, very difficult time for me. I was asked in obedience to do something that I did not know how to do. I knew the people, and I loved the students, but I didn't know anything about being a principal." She stayed for two years as principal and then asked the mother general to remove her. Another sister was sent to be principal, and [this sister] became assistant principal, which she said was much better for her.

Sister Josephine taught first or second grade for nineteen years before she was asked to be a principal. She said, "The principal experience was very difficult because I really didn't know what to do. They kept saying, 'You're such a good teacher that you'll know what to do. You'll be able to do it.' I was a good primary teacher. I struggled [as principal] for three years. I stayed on for another ten years, but not as principal, and had wonderful experiences."

Sister Martin Joseph was a young principal, twenty-nine years old, of a school mostly staffed with older sisters. She said, "They told me in no ill words they weren't doing a thing that they didn't want to because they were old enough to be my grandmother. So I called the superior. She said, 'I put you there because I think you can handle it.' It was miserable with the teachers, but it was wonderful with the kids."

Then Sister Martin Joseph was given another surprise. She said, "We were in a meeting, and Sister Eleanor called me over and said, 'I have some news for you, Sister. (This was in October.) I've already talked with Monsignor, and you're going to have to be changed at the end of two years because he has other plans for you.'" Sister Martin Joseph was asked to finish her master's degree at Catholic University (she only had one semester left). Then she was asked to start the library at the University of Dallas. She said, "I hadn't had any experience." They said, "Bishop Gorman and I have talked it over, and we think you can do it. So do it!" Sister added, "God just opens a door and shoves you through it." She started the library at the University of Dallas and then at Nolan High School. She later served as a librarian and archivist in New York. When she retired to Texas, she worked as a volunteer archivist at Texas Christian University and archivist for the Sisters of St. Mary.

LEARNING ON THE JOB

Most of the sisters learned to be principal the same way they learned to be teachers—by doing the job with the help of the older sisters. They usually had no clerical help, and most of them taught while serving as principal. Sister Teresa said that she finished her bachelor's degree by correspondence from Our Lady of the Lake and then waited three years before she went back to get her master's. But she said, "I was still the principal all this time. Actually it was pretty good because I think I got a lot more out of my administration courses and education courses because I knew what they were talking about from experience. I remember the summer when I was taking a class called 'The School Principal.' I walked into that class, and the professor said, 'Haven't you had this class?' I said, 'No. I've had the job, but I haven't had the class.'"

Sister St. John was made an elementary school principal right after she made perpetual vows. She was also teaching seventh and eighth grade. She said she didn't have a whole lot of time to get into mischief or worry about anything. Some of the teachers were older and more experienced than she, but she said they were very supportive. She shared the example of Sister Wilfred, who was a master teacher and was over sixty years old. Sister St. John wasn't sure how she could be principal with a teacher so much older and more experienced, but one day when Sister Wilfred was really down on the students, she asked Sister St. John to come in and talk to them. That evening Sister Wilfred said, "I was pushing down on those flowers, and you sprinkled them." Sister St. John said, "For a woman of her reputation, with her age and experience, to say that to a twenty-six-year old, you know . . . community life was incredible. And I think whatever I have and whatever I am, except for the first seventeen years, came through this community." She later said, "You know, all along the way there have been such fine women."

In 1960 Sister Francesca was sent to California. She said,

> I was asked to be principal, and I had no background for being principal. I was teaching first grade, had sixteen classrooms, and four hundred and some children. We had eight sisters in the convent, and I was in charge of that. I was in my early forties, and I got through it real well. We were the happiest group of sisters. They were all older than I except for one. The teachers were very supportive of me. I went to school early, saw them in the morning, and then went to my classroom. If they had any problems or problem children, they would send them to me, and I'd put them in the back of the classroom. Sometimes I'd give them a job, then I'd send them back later in the day. The Lord surely helped me, and I just had to trust that things would work out, and I bluffed my way through. No matter where I went, what convent or school, there has always been someone around me who could help me.

Sister Mary M. described learning to be a principal: "The principal said, 'Meet with me, and I will go over things with you.' So I met with her one day and we spent the entire day. She handed over the keys, this big [key ring]. She went key by key and told me what they were for. That was the in-service." Sister Mary said that it was one of the mothers who really taught her the things she needed to know. "I remember registration and the first school board meeting. The mother came and she said, 'Did you get any money, some change for the registration?' I said, 'Do I need any money?' She said, 'Why don't you let me go down and cash you a check.' I didn't even know about that. My secretary was brand new too, and she was kind of afraid."

Sister Mary said, "The first two weeks of school, one of the sisters on the staff had a mental breakdown, so I had to cope with that. But I loved the school; I absolutely loved it. I loved the people. They wanted an education for their children so badly. Most of them were manual workers, and they wanted their children to have more. That was my first principalship. I grew a lot during that time. Before then I had taught in many of our schools. I think they really taught me a lot about what to do and what not to do."

Sister Bernice became a principal in an interesting school.

> It was, I guess, 90 percent Hispanic. I think that I did teach the children, and I worked with the faculty, but I think the people there taught me. It was a different culture. The people were so welcoming and loving. Their whole beautiful culture was there. They taught me so much. While I was there, I began to see a little bit of an overlap between communities. You have your community at school, and we have community in our congregation. Some of those skills that we had learned could be used to be taken over to this other community; [for example] the whole idea of trying to work together, trying not to have people at odds. You might say, "Everybody knows that," but in those days not everybody knew that. [I met] with the individual teachers and tried to see what their best qualities were because evidently that had been done for me. I think it was that looking at the whole person, looking at each

individual teacher, taking time, having fun events for the teachers. I was trying to bring some of the things we were doing in community over to the school.

As always in those days, Sister Bernice was principal before she had the academic preparation for the job. She was given two years to attend university and complete her degree. She lived in an apartment for the first time, managed a checkbook for the first time, and had a car for the first time. Living in an apartment and being part of a parish brought her into contact with lay people, including a professor and his wife and some people from Thailand. Sister Bernice described that experience as "a whole opening up for me."

After Sister Bernice finished her graduate work and returned to Fort Worth, the only principal position available was at OLV. She took the position but did not live there because she had learned that when the principal lives on the premises people come to the door "at all times of the day and night." Sister Bernice said that one thing she liked about that school was that it was very ethnically and socioeconomically mixed. She said, "I think that's how the real world is."

When she left OLV, Sister Bernice became associate superintendent for the diocese at the same time that she was on the council for the Sisters of St. Mary. She noted, "I think my gift was community, making people feel a part of where they were working. [I tried] to be very supportive of the principal, and when things were not quite right, the superintendent and I tried to see what we could do to make it right. Then at the diocese I was getting to know all those people and seeing their expertise and how they fit. . . . And so I can say that my gifts were used and I was enjoying it. But the part I was enjoying the most . . . was going out to the schools." Sister Bernice left the diocesan position when she was asked to go to an elementary school as an assistant principal and then principal.

Sister Bernice said that it is important to know when it is time to leave a place. Sometimes the sister does not see that it is time for her to leave; if she is lucky, the superior sees it and asks her to move. Sister Teresa was grateful that when she didn't know, the superior did. She said, "There have been some trying times, but for the most part, I've been very happy. I remember one time specifically when the decision was made for us to leave [a school]. I asked permission to stay on one more year until we could find somebody to replace me." Her request was refused, and she went to be principal of a school in another town. She said,

> It was about the middle of my first year that, looking back, I saw that was the best thing that could have happened—for me to get out of there. I wrote a letter to her and the council, thanking them for moving me because I felt like if I had not moved, I would have left the community and/or been an alcoholic. It all started as social drinking, but I had gotten to where anytime I would get a little down, I would start drinking. It wasn't until I got away from that, that I was able to see that if God hadn't moved me out of that situation, I don't know what would have happened, but I felt like it would have been either or both of those things.

PIECES COMING TOGETHER

Sister Mary F. was sent to school to study social work because she wanted to work with the poor. She said, "Within my classes over there, I became aware of the tremendous impact that good Catholic schools could have. So the pieces just kind of fell in place for me, which has been my life." She was asked to be assistant superintendent of the Catholic schools. She said, "I would take the position under two conditions. One was if they had a diocesan advisory board. I told him, 'The board has to hire me, and I have to have permission to conduct a survey to find out what . . . the people want at Catholic schools or do they want to close them' because Catholic schools were closing all over the country in 1970."

Sister conducted the survey and found that parents send their kids to a Catholic school for a number of reasons, but the most important one for the parents was a sense of community, a feeling of belonging, of being known, and of people caring about them. The survey indicated that the parents wanted to keep the schools, but they wanted more say in them. Sister Mary said, "We came up with a system of an elected policy-making school board in every school, and a diocesan board of education that was policymaking. It was kind of like the electoral college with the president. Every school had electors that they would send, and they would campaign for people to be elected to the diocesan board."

Sister also noted, "The Catholic Church, for better or for worse, is not a democracy. But Bishop Cassata was the bishop then, and he had been at the Vatican Council, which gave those participants a sense of church. We took this information to the bishop, and Bishop Cassata agreed that the decisions of the diocesan board of education would be his decisions. While I was superintendent, he never failed to sign a policy passed by the diocesan board of education."

When Bishop Cassata was replaced, the new bishop did not agree to this way of governing the schools. Sister Mary said, "People have to do what they think is right," but this difference was one of the heartaches for her. Under Bishop Cassata, she said, "The principal was hired and could be fired by the board, not by the pastor. It was the board that made the policies, not the pastor. Now, the board could make mistakes, but the board was more likely to make good decisions as a group than a priest who had had no training at all in running a school. So the pastor was important to the school, but the burden of running a school was not on the shoulders of the pastor. That's the way the bishop and I both saw it."

When the new bishop came in, this system was changed. Sister said, "Within the first year, he made all boards into advisory bodies, which meant that the pastor was head of the school. By this time I was superintendent." After a year, she realized that this was not a workable situation for her, and she resigned. She said,

When I resigned, Bishop Delaney was really not happy because I didn't resign to him; I resigned to the board. He had hired somebody without discussion with the diocesan board of education. He wanted me to continue as superintendent, but he wanted somebody else to be director of education. He called me up in Seattle and told me about this. He said, "I want you to continue as superintendent." I said, "Well, Bishop, I cannot tell you right now what I will do." I immediately knew what I was going to do, but I wasn't going to resign to him. So I came back, and I asked the president of the board to call a special meeting of the board, and I submitted my resignation to the board and not to Bishop Delaney. He was really, really unhappy about it. I explained to the board. I said, "In the Baltimore Catechism, there was a triangle drawn. That was the church, and you had the pope, and you had the bishops, the priests, and the people. I believe in the triangular church, but I think it's upside down." You know, when a priest is ordained and the bishop is ordained, they lie down on the floor as a symbol of their service to the people of God. It's hard for us to remember that—it really is. It was hard for all of us. But the laity can help us remember if we give them the authority to help us remember. So I resigned, and I had no idea what I was going to do. That was in August, and I resigned "as of now" when I met with the board.

One of Sister Mary F's accomplishments when she was superintendent was Cassata Learning Center, which is described on the private school web site as "a non-traditional academic environment in which the student is respected and expectations are high. Cassata's mission is to provide effective quality education that enables students of all backgrounds to raise their educational level or complete their secondary education."[2] Sister Mary said,

> Sister Bonaventure and I had attended a conference in Cincinnati where Mother Theresa had taught. At supper that night, she was sitting at a table over by herself, a little table for four, just sitting there by herself. I said, "Bonnie, let's go over there and sit by Mother Theresa." We went over and talked. She said, "You know, you don't have to go to India to find poor

2. "Cassata Learning Center."

people." Bonnie had taught at Our Mother of Mercy here in Fort Worth, and we knew well that there were poor people. (By this time I'd hired Bonnie as the assistant superintendent.) We said, "Let's start a program in the old Laneri [school] building. Let's get that building fixed up and let's have a school for kids that Nolan [the local Catholic high school] doesn't serve." So, we started Cassata Learning Center. That was in August. The building was in terrible shape. We got permission from the board and the bishop to use the building if we could get the money. We got money from the Sid Richardson Foundation and borrowed money from the diocese. We got the building fixed up. We wanted to start it in January. A monsignor on the Nolan board at the time said, "It's a good idea. But you're not going to start it in January." That was just enough to make us determined to open in January.

Sister Mary is no longer working for the diocese, but Cassata Learning Center is still serving the children of Fort Worth.

Sonia Nieto wrote about the "Catholic school effect," which she describes as schools that produce very successful students even though they are overcrowded, under-resourced, and have a less differentiated curriculum.[3] She attributes the unusual success to the "school structures that imply high expectations for all students." That certainly is part of the answer, but in schools run by the Sisters of St. Mary, I suspect that it is the deep caring of the sisters for their students, rooted in the sense of mission that makes teaching a vocation rather than just a job.

---

3. Nieto, *Affirming Diversity*, 273.

Chapter 3

Global Citizens, Missionary Sisters

"One would think it would be a fairly simple matter to define missionary work, to describe it, to explain its meaning, its purpose, and the methods by which it must be carried out."[1] Father Donovan wrote those words over twenty-five years ago, and they still ring true today. For some of us, the term "missionary" brings to mind movie images of Bible-toting foreigners trying to convert native people or large compounds in which native children were educated. For others it may bring back vague memories of saving coins to bring to school in support of the missions. Most of us probably have a sketchy conception that some religious sisters work in foreign missions but do have not much understanding of what they do or how they live.

The oldest missionary I interviewed was ninety-three at the time of the interview and was still living in the mission country. Her name was Sister Benita, and she was a missionary from Ireland to the United States. I had thought of missionaries going from the United States, but talking with her was the first time that I realized that missionaries came to the United States.

Sister Benita explained the need that led to the Irish missionaries coming here: "Many Catholics from the countries in Europe had moved here to live. When they moved here, there was no church to go to on Sunday. There was no such thing as a Catholic school. The

---

1. Donovan, *Christianity Rediscovered*, 3.

parents were working, and they didn't have time to teach the children their faith. They taught them a little, but they were growing up and abandoning their faith because they had no real instruction in it. So that was really my reason for coming to Texas."

Some of the sisters I interviewed had missionary experiences for a period of time, while other sisters went to the missions and planned to remain there for the rest of their lives. Some were nurses, some were teachers, and some went as novices, helping out where they could. All, in one way or another, were catechists. Those who stayed for long periods left the United States at a relatively young age and lived in the culture and among the people of the mission land for most of their lives. They made brief visits to the United States but were largely formed as adults by the land in which they lived. Some expressed a sense of having no culture or of being a "global citizen." They did not feel like a full citizen of the mission country or of the United States. Their ties were to the sisters in the mission countries with whom they had a shared history, yet they were still tied to the sisters in the United States who had been part of their initial formation and who were still very much their sisters.

The younger sisters I interviewed were missionaries in a time when the idea of mission was a fluid concept, changing along with the life of the church. Sister Rosemary wrote about the way that the understanding of mission has changed through the years and, within that context, how her own experience of mission changed. She said, "The 'missionary' thrust in which I have been blessed to live and to serve has been diverse and changing, as has the life of the church, of religious life, and ultimately of the world."

There were many interesting stories from the sisters who served in mission countries. I have chosen three to include here in some detail: Sister Rosemary was a missionary to Africa and Brazil during the emergence of liberation theology; Sister Charles Marie was a missionary to Africa and was living in Rwanda during the genocide; and Sister Gabriella was a missionary to Mexico who continued her work with Mexican Americans in the United States.

SISTER ROSEMARY: MISSIONARY IN AFRICA AND BRAZIL

Sister Rosemary arrived in the Democratic Republic of Congo (Congo) in 1971, which she described as "a time of 'birthing pains' in Africa and in a certain sense the church and the world." She joined a large international community of sisters from Congo, Rwanda, United States, Canada, England, and Belgium. "We were part of a large mission compound at Djuma sur le Kwilu in the tropical forest in the province of Bandundu." At the mission the sisters maintained a large girls' school, while the Jesuits administered the boys' school on the other side of the large mission church. There was a hospital, an orphanage, and numerous catechumens spent part of the year at the mission where they were instructed in the Catholic faith and rendered service as their contribution to the upkeep of the mission complex."

The Sisters of St. Mary of Namur were able to receive African religious vocations beginning in 1956, and by 1969 there were sixty-four native African sisters. Thus the mission complex included a large community of temporary professed and young religious women in the period of formation.

Sister Rosemary spent a year there. She knew very little French, and everything in the community was in French. She said, "So here I was this new person, extremely lonely, trying to learn French and wanting to do something. I could do a lot of manual labor. I took care of the library; I cleaned the dorm; I did all that kind of stuff. I had a lot of time to read. I was teaching myself French. I got a sense of simplicity, of living close to the people in a certain way. I was young. I was only twenty years old at the time, so it was all an adventure."

Sister learned French and made her requests to stay, a year at a time. As she said, "It just went on and on. I never came back." In 1973 she had the opportunity to be part of the foundation of a small community of sisters in the French-speaking part of

Cameroon. Sister described it as "kind of an experimental type of small community in the middle of the forest near a village of sixty people."

Sister Rosemary talked about the "forward-looking, visionary and courageous women who were Sisters of St. Mary." One of these women was Mother Elizabeth, a Belgian. As Sister Rosemary left Belgium for Congo, Mother Elizabeth told her, "Go and live *fraternellement* with the African sisters." This indicates the spirit and direction in which the mission countries were moving: to go and be with, live among, and minister with the native sisters.

She commented about her experience,

> As a young sister, living side by side in community with sisters from different countries of the northern hemisphere and from Africa, I had a unique experience of a new way of living in a mission country. Together we were growing into religious life within our international congregation. We were exposed to the richness as well as to the demands of living in communities that were at the same time signs of and small cells of the universal church, attempting to make God's kingdom more visible in the world. We became increasingly conscious of the importance of providing space and possibilities for the people of the different African countries in which we ministered to have the freedom of religious expressions "welling up" from their own culture.

It was a big change from the idea of mission in a large mission compound to the idea of living in a small village, sharing the lifestyle of the people, and living among them. It meant cooking over a wood fire, washing their clothes at a natural water source in the forest, and carrying buckets of water up from there for their daily needs. This was only the second community the province established for this purpose. In Cameroon they began as a community of three sisters: a Congolese, a Belgian, and an American. They started a small dispensary, taught in a preschool, and helped with religion classes in the nearby grade school.

THE ARMS OF GOD

After six years in the Democratic Republic of Congo, Cameroon, and Rwanda, Sister Rosemary went to Latin America, a place in which she said, "The desire of our congregation and the call of the church in Latin America coincided." After a four-month language and cultural initiation, Sister was sent to Poco Verde, a small town in the interior of the state of Sergipe to join the four sisters who had founded the community the previous year.

SISTERS IN BRAZIL

On the day of the arrival of the first sisters in the parish of St. Sebastian a few months earlier, the local bishop introduced them saying among other things to the people: "These are the missionary Sisters of St. Mary. From now on they are our Brazilian sisters in Christ. They have come to evangelize, to help the population, to assist the priest in his task, and to help the Christians to better pray and live."

Sister Rosemary said that the transit sign *Pare, olhe, ver* ("stop, look, listen") that they learned in the intensive language training program became symbols for what they tried to put into practice. She said,

> After the Second Vatican Council, missionary activity as I have experienced it in our congregation has put even more emphasis on validating and respecting the spiritual, religious, and human treasures inherent within a particular people. As we moved into a new part of the American continent, we have striven to go slowly, to watch, and to listen before undertaking a ministry or service for the people. The way of mission has been very much one of solidarity, especially with the marginalized, the less privileged of this world, of living among them and helping them to develop their capacities to the fullest. We have tried to listen and to look at what is being lived in the local church and in the faith lives of the people.

Donovan said that "mission was conceived not only as the proclamation of the gospel but also as a commitment to justice, genuine development, and liberation of the human person from every oppressive situation."[2] In Brazil the sisters noticed the vast illiteracy and, in response, created literacy schools, first for the children and then for the adults. Sister Rosemary told about a neighbor named Clotilde who attended these literacy classes and was later trained by the sisters, "Afterwards she taught as an excellent teacher in that same school. Twenty-five years later Clotilde, who was born into a very poor, hard-working family, has a masters degree in education and works for the Education Department on the state level. She continues to send financial help to her family and shares her gift with her own people through education."

Sister Rosemary talked about how the sisters became a part of the communities in which they lived and formed very close bonds with the people. She said, "Living as close to them as we do, we share in their daily struggles, their joys, and their sorrows. This sharing goes in both directions. At the time of September 11, 2001, I was in Tobias Barreto in Sergipe, where I have lived for many years. The day after we learned of the tragedy, people came to our house; others stopped us on the street. One man had tears in his eyes as he told me how sorry he was and hoped that none of my family was a victim."

She said, "We were celebrating twenty-five years of that foundation, and I just happened to be back in that house, and so the people wanted to have some type of celebration for us for being in that parish for twenty-five years. We really wanted it to be a type of evangelization opportunity as well, and there had been a lot of violence in that area and drugs and street children." The planning for the celebration was soon after September 11, 2001, when the president was saying that the United States might go into Iraq. The Sisters of St. Mary are committed to nonviolence, so these sisters decided to include nonviolence and peace as part of this celebration. Sister said, "The anniversary was November 19, so from September till then, a group of us worked, sisters and lay persons,

2. Donovan, *Christianity Rediscovered*, 3.

preparing all sorts of plans, lesson plans to be given in schools, activities with the adults, faith sharing, and some services that we had in church. It was all going to culminate on the nineteenth with a peace walk. We had games, contests, and all sorts of things. We got the kids to do posters and projects, and they put on shows in their schools. It was just incredible. We did the groundwork, and it just exploded."

She added that they were going to have a peace walk from a village fifteen miles away to their town, stopping for moments of prayer along the way. For example, one of the stops was in front of the penitentiary, where they prayed for "those who were imprisoned as well as their victims and those who had suffered because of the violence outside of the prison and within."

The peace walk started at 6:30 a.m. because the temperature would probably reach the high nineties. The sisters had no idea whether anyone would show up to walk and pray with them. Sister Rosemary said, "By noontime we arrived in front of the church, and there were over three thousand people. Now this you just have to imagine. It was a small town. There are probably about fifteen thousand people in town, but there were buses that came from surrounding villages bringing people to participate. The mayor and people from other political parties were all in the march." Sister further explained that one day before the walk she had gone to the house of a teacher in one of the schools to speak with her. Her son, a student in the preschool/kindergarten class, looked at Sister and told his mother, 'Look, Mama! Peace!'"

The sisters stood for peace in this village. Another woman, whom the sisters had known since she was a teenager, had a five-year-old whose school had been working with them about saying "no" to violence and how to treat others. One day, Sister was meeting with parents of the first communion group that included this boy. The mother said that she and her husband argued a lot and that they were arguing one night when the five-year-old girl came up to them and said, "You'd better stop fighting. Don't you know we're supposed to be non-violent?"

The street where the sisters lived was in an area of extreme poverty. The woman across the street had six children, and one of them attended the literacy school run by the sisters. The family was very poor and did not always have enough to eat. Sister Rosemary said that she went over to the house one day and saw Jacqueline, the young child who was supposed to be attending literacy school. Sister asked if Jacqueline was sick. The mother said that she was not sick, but that she didn't have anything to give her to eat that morning, so she did not send her to school. Sister Rosemary brought over some groceries for the family from the sisters' house. The woman's brother lived out in the country. The mother came to the sisters' house on market day with three pieces of fresh corn and she said, "Sister, my brother brought six pieces of corn today from his farm, and I wanted you all to have three pieces." She had brought them half of what she had.

Sister Rosemary summed up her experience as follows:

> You're led to engage with life and people that are there at the time and the situation. I was afraid the first time I had to go talk about the book of Genesis in front of one hundred adults in Portuguese using a microphone. Somehow you do it. Sometimes I'd be in Brazil and I'd stop and think, "Here I am in the middle of this little town, in the middle of the northeastern part of Brazil, in this poor insignificant area, and people who couldn't care less what happens in the next election, who loses their job and who doesn't, and all that. You know, that's just the little bit of the world you're in right now, you know, engaging with life."

Sister Rosemary came home for a visit every three years and was home for two years for sabbatical. During that time she finished her bachelor's degree and then went back to Brazil. In all, she was thirty-three years out of the country. In 2003 she agreed to return to help the three young women who were from other nationalities who were ready to begin a formation program with the

Sisters of St. Mary. She is working with students at Nolan (a local Catholic high school) and earned her master's degree in theological studies from Brite Divinity School in Fort Worth.

Sister described her return to the United States: "There is always a certain tension within because of those formative years in my life that I lived out of the country. My value system and world vision differ from many people here among whom I live who have not experienced the same thing. And so on a certain level there are presumptions and a seeming lack of connection with some community members who cannot relate to my past reality, which has greatly influenced me. On the other hand, some persons in and even outside the community seem to have a greater perception of the two worlds of which I am a part."

Missionary sisters may have missed too many shared experiences to ever feel fully a part of the culture to which they have returned. On the other hand, these sisters, even when they live very closely with the people, are never truly part of the missionary country and culture. Sister Rosemary talked about the fact that when she was in Congo, she never thought about the fact that she wasn't black. It became clear to her when the Congolese sisters came to the mission for the funeral of a priest. She said, "When Sister Mary Bruno introduced me to them and said that I was the assistant novice mistress, they looked at me and said, 'Well, we sure hope the novice mistress is Congolese.'" She added, "After awhile you kind of live in the middle of others who don't think you're different. When you're in Brazil, you think you're Brazilian, and you accept the mentality. There's a kind of poverty in knowing that you'll never be one of them."

It is no surprise that Sister said that she sometimes feels like "a man without a country" but also like a global citizen because she has life experience that has led to her awareness of the effects of the lifestyle of people in America on the lives of the common poor person walking down the street in the northeastern part of Brazil. She simultaneously lives with a global sense and a sense of not completely belonging to any place. The gift of this awareness is that Sister has become "a kind of bridge builder for people who want a connection to that world and people who have just responded to having met me with this incredible generosity for our missions."

SISTER CHARLES MARIE IN CONGO AND RWANDA: MISSIONARIES IN TROUBLED TIMES

She doesn't look like a hero. She is a small woman with a voice so quiet that my recorder did not pick it up. In that same soft, quiet voice, she speaks of experiences beyond my imagination. There were times when it seemed as if she were there, in Rwanda, reporting what she was seeing, not sitting in the parlor years later remembering and telling me about it. At those times, her voice became distant, and it was as if she took me there with her. I, who had never been to Africa or witnessed genocide, was there, sitting on the bench by the forest, hearing the screams and tasting the fear. She does not speak of these things as if they are extraordinary but as if they just are.

Sister Charles Marie speaks of herself as a woman of "two vocations." The first was her entrance into religious life one week after graduating from college. This was a long way for the young woman who grew up in a small town of about three hundred people. Her family was the only Catholic family in town at the time, and all of her schooling was in public schools. She could not make her first communion until sixth grade because she was not able to prepare for it. This belated first communion became significant. Charles Marie said, "The Eucharist was the beginning of a strong attachment to Christ."

When she was fifteen, she spent the summer with her grandmother in a town in which there was a Catholic church. She said, "I felt irresistibly drawn to daily Mass. I didn't understand much about the deep meaning of the Eucharist, but I had a simple faith in the presence of Jesus in Communion. It was at this time that I began feeling a strong invitation to religious life." She seemed to forget about this experience her senior year in high school, but as she continued through college it surfaced again. She began to feel drawn to the Eucharist again and attended daily Mass as often as she could. She said, "Toward the end of my college years, the idea of religious life became a pressing question for me. I remember well the day when a 'yes!' appeared strongly within me. From then on, I never doubted." She thought she was entering religious life to be close to Jesus and live out a life with him. This young, small-town woman, who was shocked by the college town of thousands of students, had no idea that she would spend most of her religious life far from home and live through one of the worst genocides since World War II. She said, "The decision for me to go to Africa was made on Holy Saturday, and the alleluias of Easter had a very special meaning for me on that day."

She was to leave at the end of the school year for what turned out to be thirty-eight years alternating between Rwanda and Congo. There was a special departure Mass for her with the antiphon "The Lord is my rock, all my strength is in him," which was composed by one of the sisters. Sister Charles Marie said, "All night long in the train on the way to Chicago, I was singing that song in my heart as the tears rolled down."

BEGINNING OF MISSIONARY LIFE

She arrived at Kigali on the morning of August 10, 1964. Then she drove through the beautiful hills of Rwanda and arrived at Mubuga in late afternoon. That is where her missionary life began.

Over the next thirty-eight years, she taught (mostly religion, English, and music) and was novice director for seventeen years at four different intervals. For the last eight years, she was responsible for a community of junior sisters who studied at several universities in Kinshasa, Congo.

Sister Charles Marie made her perpetual vows in 1965 at the Church of Mubuga at a mass prepared by herself and her students. She said, "This was my 'yes' to the Lord forever and, I believe, the confirmation of my call to Africa."

In Mubuga the sisters taught in a secondary school, working to elevate the status of women. When I asked about that, she said that it is one of the charisms of her congregation, which had been in Africa since the 1920s. She said of the beginning of her missionary life, "All was new." Her fears about learning languages seemed real since she appeared to have forgotten the French she had learned in Belgium. As she spoke about the beauty of the hills, her face lit up as if she were seeing it again in her mind's eye. Then in the next breath she spoke of the terrible poverty of the people, and those same eyes softened with sadness. They had one hundred and sixty boarders, no water, and too little space. The dining room was so small that they had to eat each meal in two parts. The girls would be going back and forth from the stream to get water several times a day (and not willingly). Sister Charles Marie drove to the markets nearby or to the city to get food for the students. She said that this was difficult because of the condition of the roads; it took a long time to go a short distance.

One of the themes of Sister Charles Marie's missionary life is that she has always ended up dealing with materials such as money and buildings. When she laughingly spoke of that, it was in a good-natured way as one might speak of a stray dog that finds a way to follow you home just when you think you have outrun it. This diminutive woman learned to draw plans, order supplies, hire labor, and supervise the construction of buildings. She was treasurer for the Congo and did much buying, shipping out, and other kinds of business for the six communities in the interior of the country.

When I asked Sister Charles Marie how she was able to do all of these things—for example, how she could build buildings when she had no background in construction—she said that she did it like she did everything: "because it needed to be done." She would look at me with surprise when I asked her about such things, as if it had not occurred to her to wonder if she could do it. Her life, in many ways, is captured by this sense of obedience to what needs to be done.

FOUNDATIONS

Sister Charles Marie wrote in April 2004, "When I think back on the evolution of our history in Africa, I think of the stories of our foundations. I was fortunate to have participated in six of them between 1964 and 1978. For the most part, our orientation at that time was to move out of institutions into small vibrant communities closer to the population. It was primarily a desire to bring Christ into places where he was less known and to help young women in their human and spiritual development." She continued,

> Each detail was considered important and purposeful. Surprises always modified our plans.
>
> The preparation of Rusasa is a vivid memory for me. It was in a faraway corner of the country where only 20 percent of the population had been exposed to Christianity. That point was definitely an attraction for us. Our first visit was unforgettable. It was an extremely primitive village, quite different from what was familiar to us in other parts of Rwanda. The needs . . . were immense. It all seemed so ripe for a fruitful apostolate.
>
> As we were searching for a decision, we just happened upon the story in the Acts of the Apostles where Paul and Barnabas were traveling in one direction and the Holy Spirit guided them in another. This fired us up so much that we went back for a second visit to Rusasa, and everything about it seemed just exactly what Dom Minsart and Mother Claire [the founders of the Sisters of St. Mary of Namur] would have wanted for us. From that point on, there was no stopping us on that project. The audacity of this undertaking was astonishing as I look back on it. There is no doubt that it was beautiful while it lasted. The war drove our sisters from there in January 1992.

As I ponder these experiences, I think of a friend of mine in Rwanda. When a sister lamented the fact that her dispensary had been completely destroyed by hostility, Maria responded with these powerful words: "Yes, your building was destroyed, but nothing can destroy the love you put into it while caring for the sick for so many years."

EVANGELIZATION

Sister Charles Marie worked in Congo, where the Sisters of St. Mary of Namur had worked since 1923 trying to bring Jesus into the lives of many, trying to educate young women. She said,

> My experience in this began in a memorable way while I was a young novice director in Djuma. An important part of the novices' formation was to experience evangelization. In our parish there were about a hundred and fifty villages to be served at that time. Many catechists worked out of the parish with this intention, but we sisters (generally four including an experienced Congolese sister, two novices, and myself) had a special four-day retreat program for the villages that were ready for the sacraments. This retreat consisted of a special time of formation and prayer for all age groups. On Sunday the priest would come for the Eucharist and the sacraments: baptisms, marriages, etc. The people provided us with a place to sleep and also food. In the evenings we would sit outside with the people and listen to them talk, sing, and dance. I must admit that these evenings in the moonlight, listening to the people's stories, taught me quite a lot. I think back on this as real mission experience.

TROUBLED TIMES IN RWANDA

Sister Charles Marie also experienced what she called "troubled times." She said,

> In 1971 there were uneasy times in Congo, so we moved the novices to Rwanda. In 1973, when I was in Kigali to welcome a Bible specialist for a Bible session, we woke up one morn-

ing in the midst of a coup d'état. The government had been overthrown. The town was full of tanks and soldiers. We were unable to leave Kigali for a few days. That was followed by a period of relative normalcy for seventeen years.

Everything changed on October 1, 1990, when the war began in Rwanda. The pope had just left . . . when the country was attacked on its northern border. Sister Jean Benoit had just arrived for her first visit. She was blocked in Mubuga for ten days. A sister had an operation in Kabgayi and could not return. We couldn't get out of Kiruhura without a special paper for every single move we would make. I spent many hours standing in line trying to get permission to travel.

In 1991 the rebel forces came into Rwanda from Uganda, forcing the sisters to evacuate from Rusasa, the border community. The sisters left Rusasa with all the people. Sister M. Damien, a beautiful Rwandan sister, was the last to leave as she was delivering a local woman's baby. After this evacuation, she worked with these displaced Rwandans in Mwange until the situation got very dangerous there as well. We went to get her in the midst of heavy cannon fire. She was made responsible for a health center in the east of our country. A few months later at the age of thirty-five, she was killed in a bus accident. It was a terrible loss for us all. People from all over Rwanda came down to Kiruhura for her funeral. There were all kinds of people of both races, and some were political leaders. One of these from a faraway town stood up in the crowd and said, "We just wanted to tell you we loved her."

Sister Damien had worked with everyone with the same care and love without ever making any distinction of race or other differences. This sister, now buried beside our chapel in Kiruhura, lives on as a powerful witness of a Universal Spirit.

After awhile, things seemed to ease up in the rest of the country, but the war went on and came to a climax in April 1994 when the airplane of the president of Rwanda was shot down. At this time the genocide began, and we lived through the three months of terror that has filled the news.

Sister talked about the sound of gunfire and cannons that could be heard from their house. She said, "It was like being in prison . . . day after day—the anguish and always being threatened

—it was terribly hard." It was the rainy season. Sister said with a look of wonder in her eyes that each day there was enough rain to fill the water tank for the needs of that day. Each day they would go out to the garden and harvest all of the edible food. Then the next day, again, there was just enough water and food for a day, and in that way the Lord provided." She continued,

> There was the anguish of our sisters who were losing family members but never knowing what was happening to them. We were living that loss too. Also there were militiamen all around our house prohibiting people from hiding on our property. When we left food hidden for people out in the bushes around our house, they would find them and take them out and slaughter them. There was an elderly man who had been a night watchman for us for twenty years. He was like a father to us. But we couldn't hide him; we couldn't protect him. If it had been just me, it would be one thing, but I couldn't risk the lives of those [sisters] for whom I was responsible. It was very frustrating. Some days we heard the cries of people being slaughtered very near us. One day it was especially terrible. During the night there was a bad rainstorm. As I was lying on my bed thinking of these people half dead out in the rain, the only thing that could console me was the image of a beautiful icon of the resurrection in which Jesus is holding out his hand to Adam and pulling him out of the underworld into eternal life.
>
> In spite of our living faith, there was fear that we would be next. (We knew that all of the sisters in another community a few miles away had been killed—many congregations were not spared). We felt that the Lord . . . taught us many things during those hard times. For example, we learned that you can lose everything—personal things, material things—and it doesn't matter too much.
>
> In the group of twenty-six people that made up our community in April, May, and June, more than half was Tutsi, and they especially were in serious danger. They stayed inside, as inconspicuous as possible, and the others did the outside jobs, relations, etc. Our Hutu sisters were considerate and loveable. They also had suffered terribly from this, but in a different way than the Tutsis, who were literally awaiting death every day

(as we all were to a certain extent). Every morning, we would get up and wonder, "Lord, is it today?"

After April 6 we had no apostolic activities; we were not allowed to help the Tutsis who were being persecuted, which was painfully frustrating. It seemed to us that our only reasons for being were the glory of God and being a witness to the fact that it is possible to live together in real charity (and this at great cost).

The first weeks with its terrors of the nights and days went by with a desperate clinging to Christ in prayer together with many hours of adoration. As the days went by, there was a time of perseverance—a struggle not to slip or to let go. It was a very nerve-wracking experience to say the least.

There were checkpoints, and although Sister said that the soldiers were not mean to them, the experience of being repeatedly stopped and questioned at gunpoint was difficult. Sister told of a priest who was diabetic and couldn't get medicine, so he just died. The pastor asked her to take the priest's things to another town. On this trip she was stopped at a checkpoint, and they went through all of the priest's things. She finally told them that they were rifling through the belongings of a dead man.

She continued,

> The sisters wore everything they valued. Some kept their diplomas under the back of their shirts. They might wear several blouses and skirts. They divided up the money in the house so that each had some in case they were separated. Every day, at any moment, some faithful neighbors might give us a signal that the militiamen were coming to loot, to kill, or both. Our sisters would bury things and run and hide in the woods all day long, hoping that these "visitors" would be satisfied with only looting and go away. The forest wasn't thick, just a beautiful woods a short distance from the house, but it made them feel more secure to hide there. Two times some local authority just happened by and stopped the militiamen. We experienced many such miracles. God who is mighty was doing great things for us.

Hiding in the forest was not foolproof, and one day the soldiers came and rounded up the sisters they found. They put them in a group in a clearing and told them to sit there and not move. They said that they had better not be hiding anyone, or the soldiers would come back and kill them all. Of course, the sisters were hiding people. The soldiers looked around, but Sister said they didn't look too thoroughly, and then they moved on. There were many times when Sister said that the soldiers looked fierce but seemed to "go easy" on them.

Sister Charles Marie stayed closer to the house to be with a sister who walked with a cane and could not hide in the woods. She said that one day, as the lame sister and she were sitting on a bench outside, they saw the soldiers run by, hundreds of them, and they had leaves on their bodies and were carrying machetes and clubs. A bit later they heard screams, and she thought, "What am I doing sitting here while people are being hurt?" The sisters from another congregation that were hiding with them were dressed in native garb, which made them more vulnerable. The Sisters of St. Mary gave them their extra habits to wear so as to be like them.

She said, "These were times of prayer and of much charity among congregations. Everyone was doing things for each other and sharing everything . . . the little they had. Their only communication with the other communities was through short-wave radio and letters that could be sent with priests who passed through." In one case, Sister Charles Marie sent letters with a Congolese who was afraid to go through the woods and intended to go through Burundi (with a destination of Bukavu). In one of these letters, written from Kiruhura ten days after the beginning of the genocide, she wrote, "There was an envelope for you and others for my family. I hope by the goodness of God you get it." In this letter Sister Charles Marie told about how Sister Marguerite Marie got out of Kigali through providence and the Lord's love. She dared cross the city in the midst of massacres and waited four hours for a pass to leave. A Congolese priest was doing the same thing, and they left together in the priest's car. It was a difficult trip. They went all the way to Gitarama with a gun in their backs held by a drunken soldier. They gave him money and oranges. She survived with her papers in order. It was an experience that marked her.

Another sister, Sister Philothée, arrived home after having escaped Ruhengéri. She was able to get to the wheat factory at the entrance of the city. The couple in charge welcomed them, the twenty-one people that were her companions in a thirty-day retreat. They stayed five days and six nights. They had slept on the floor together in the same place.

Sister continues,

> It was Friday when everything turned dangerous. One driver took an abandoned car, and the wheat factory gave another. They followed back roads toward Gitarama. They saw places where everything was going very badly. In Kabgayi, Sister Philothée came across a bus filled with displaced people. She was able to squeeze into this bus and got off on the road in front of our house. It was already dark. She came into the back of the chapel very quietly. You can imagine how she was welcomed! She tells it all, stressing the positive side, the goodness of people everywhere, even good soldiers who helped them.
>
> The tension was heavy for everyone. Despite everything, being so close to the road wasn't very good. We tried to be inconspicuous so as not to be seen. Knowing that church people are not spared creates something radically different in your heart—the way you pray the Psalms, the words of the gospel, the way you look at one another, the attention you pay to others. The novices assumed the brutal reality of the country. They lived it together and with God. There were no secrets. Everyone made an effort to think farther than this country and to sing, to laugh, etc. The tension was tiring. We slept longer than usual.

It became clear that the sisters had to get out of Rwanda, but they did not want to leave until they got papers for the native novices and sisters. Sister Charles Marie said of the young sisters, "We asked each young sister if she wanted to return temporarily to her family. Nobody said she did."

Anxious for the safety of her sisters, the fifty-seven-year-old nun decided to drive to Butare, a neighboring town about twelve miles away to try to get the papers of each sister so they would not be considered refugees in another country. She took one of the sisters, a Hutu, with her and sped down the road. On their way back, however, they were met by a mass exodus of Hutu people coming down the road toward them. In the two hours they had been gone, the Tutsi rebels had taken Kiruhura. Members of the army stopped her. They told her that the rebels were on the hill, and if she tried to continue down the road, they would assume that the vehicle was an army vehicle and she would be shot. The Hutu sister with her suggested that they take a small road that went through the hills away from the main road as an alternate route to the house. Sister Charles Marie commented, "You can imagine, there were thousands and thousands of people on the road. I was plowing through them in my Suzuki car going the other way. We were trying to get back home, but we never did. We couldn't get through." They found two of their Hutu sisters and several aspirants who had escaped, picked them up, and returned to Butare.

They learned later that when the Tutsi rebels were closing in on Kiruhura, the local Rwandans had run through the region urging the people to get out. Some of the sisters who were Hutus ran, while those who were Tutsis knew they had to hide inside the convent. The rebels who found them eventually protected these sisters.

On leaving Butare, Sister Charles Marie and the sisters joined another congregation and made their way toward the border. Her sisters rode in the other sister's van, and Sister Charles Marie drove a man in her Suzuki. When they reached the border, Sister broke down in tears. Probably they were in part the tears not shed through the ordeal but nevertheless tears of relief. Mostly, though, she said they were tears of sadness because they had to leave the native aspirants behind since they could not get papers for them to travel. She said that she found later that the aspirants survived and were safe. At this point in her tale, Sister had to stop because the sadness was too much. She was surprised to have such an intense reaction after all this time. It seemed to me that a woman of such big heart, who had given her life to Africa, will perhaps never be able to escape the great sadness of what happened to the people there.

Sister Charles Marie and her novices who had escaped Rwanda went to Cameroon. The novices delayed their commitment to religious life a bit because everyone believed that they first needed some time to relax. As she spoke of these young "war novices" making their first vows, there was the same delight as when she spoke of her own religious life.

In a way, it was a happy ending to a very difficult story. Sister Charles Marie spoke about the "unifying action of the Holy Spirit within the body of Christ that has brought us all very close together. This is deeply felt—beyond all words." She said that the Rwandan sisters felt this love and concern very deeply. They received letters, cards, faxes, and invitations. They felt that they would be welcomed in all parts of the world. Many of them lost most of their family members or didn't know if they had or not. She said, "Our congregation is the only real family left for some of them. Our sisters all over the world were a tremendous support. All our sisters got out of Rwanda safely except five who chose to stay. We left six houses and all our ministries with hopes of going back, but the future was unknown to us."

KINSHASA

After the vows of her war novices in Cameroon, Sister Charles Marie went to Kinshasa where she had worked for eight years. In 1995 she had the mission of making a search for the families of our sisters in the refugee camps of Goma and Bukavu on the eastern border of Congo.

She related,

> In Kinshasa in 1996, there was growing animosity between Congo and Rwanda. Our Rwandan sisters were in danger,

and we were obliged to evacuate them, for their safety and the safety of all the sisters. First, they were hidden in a woman's house for a few days. During that time we prepared for their evacuation. Some Sisters of Mary dressed them in their local clothes, and we crossed town with them at night, and they hid again in a convent near the river. This was a very unpleasant experience. We got a second group out a little later, but it wasn't quite as bad.

I was absent during the victory of Kabila and his army in May 1997. In Kinshasa the sisters lived through days of anguish, but there was no all-out war in town. In August 1998, there was real war with Rwanda. This was sad for us once more because we cherished our precious internationality. There was some bombing in town at that time. I was alone with another sister. We had whole families in our convent. Millions of people were displaced, and food was very hard to find. I remember walking for a couple of hours all the way to the river to find some rice. This was when the *barrage d'Inga* [electric plant] had been damaged, and there was no water or electricity. At that time one young man told me that there were thirty people in his house with no food or water. During this time four men made several days of retreat in our chapel ... singing, praying, and fasting, while we could hear shooting all around.

In 2002 Sister made a visit to the United States. She did not expect this to be the end of her missionary life in Africa. She took a sabbatical, and at the end of it, expecting to go back, she gave away everything that did not fit into one suitcase and boarded a plane for Belgium. In Atlanta, where she was to change planes, she had a stroke. She became disoriented and did not know where she was going. Airline officials notified the congregation and helped her to return to Fort Worth. She still has no memory of that day but is not otherwise affected by the stroke. After her recuperation, she again made plans to go to Belgium, and once more was prevented from doing so, this time by a heart problem. These events confused her because it appeared that she was not to go back, but she was not sure what she was supposed to do next. Looking back on her life, she said that until this time it was always obvious what she was to do—it was always right there in front of her. Now it was not clear.

She met a woman who teaches piano, and she began to take lessons and to play piano with her. The way she talked about it, the piano seemed to be part of Sister's soul. It was such a good and refreshing thing for her that she wondered if it was right to spend time on something that was such a delight.

It struck me as I listened to her that she is past the age when many women retire and spend a lot of their time on recreation. Nevertheless, after a time her teacher convinced her that she is gifted in this area and that she could teach lessons. She began teaching students at the school next to the house where she lives, and she is doing that with the same commitment and love that she served the young people of Africa. She has another trip planned to Belgium, and this time she is concerned to make sure that her young piano students will not be disrupted by her absence.

I asked Sister what she would want to tell young women today if she could give them a message from her lived experience. She said that she would encourage them to live in a third world country for a time. She said that it is a life-changing experience, and one can never look at things in the same way again afterwards. Sister Charles Marie still listens to the BBC world news on the radio at night to try to keep her international perspective.

She talked about the fact that when she was young and went to Congo, she had the illusion that she would become totally one of them. She said that after years there, she realized that she would never be Congolese. On the other hand, after being home in Texas for a time, she has realized she will also never be fully American again. She will never be a citizen of one country, but she will always be, with all her heart and soul, a Sister of Saint Mary of Namur, and that is what she brings with her wherever she goes.

In 2002 Sister Charles Marie wrote a personal mission statement at the end of a returned missioners workshop.

With gratitude for all the graces of my life, I consider this to be an expression of my deepest aspirations:

In the simplicity of my heart,
I desire
To radiate God's love,
To keep my heart and mind open to the whole world,
To "be with" Jesus present in the poor and neglected,
And to find my real home in Him,
Who is the same yesterday, today, and forever.

Mission accomplished, Sister Charles Marie!

MISSIONARIES TO MEXICO AND SPANISH-SPEAKING AMERICANS: SISTER GABRIELLA AND SISTER DOROTHY

Her parents were laborers whose father moved to Texas from Mexico during the revolution, while her mother was already a third-generation Texan. Sister Gabriella grew up in a barrio, surrounded by other Mexican Americans. Everyone in her elementary school spoke Spanish except for twin African American boys. Everyone had to learn to speak English in school, and at home they spoke an amalgamation of English and Spanish or "Tex Mex."

Sister Gabriella attended a Catholic grade school staffed by Sisters of the Sacred Heart where she first began to think she might want to be a sister. She was attracted at first "by the outer trappings" and an imagined but unreal way of life. She said, "It was like I fell in love with an image, not the reality." At the same time, she knew that she could not enter the convent because she needed to work and help her family. She answered an ad in the church bulletin for religion teachers one day, which allowed her to get to know the Sisters of St. Mary. Her attraction to religious life grew, but when she talked with her parents about it, they took her to speak to a priest who discouraged her so much that she didn't even mention it again for several years.

Gabriella was one of eight children, and with both parents working hard to support the family, she became "like a second mama," taking care of the house, cleaning, cooking, ironing, and doing all the housework and babysitting. She attended a technical high school because it would provide her the training necessary to do office work. She said, "The school was downtown, so I got to take the 7:10 a.m. bus every day. I remember the first time I saw different-colored people. My dad was driving the car, and a group of people were getting on the bus, and I saw a black person, and then I saw a white person, and I looked at my skin and thought, 'Well, I'm not white, and I'm not black. I am brown.' It was a moment of awakening, of awareness, of discovering differences in people."

After high school she found a job working in a one-person office. She worked for a man who had other businesses who would come in early in the morning and stay a short time, not returning until the next day. As a result, she had a lot of time alone to think about things and about her relationship with God. She said, "I would pray as I walked to the bus stop and on the bus, nourishing a hope that was probably very dim at that point." After three years she quit her job and was going to find a way to enter the Sisters of St. Mary when her dad got very sick and she felt that she couldn't continue with her plans because she needed to help support the family. She got two jobs, but she told her new boss that she intended to enter the convent as soon as she could. She said that he was an Episcopalian. He thought it was a noble cause or something, so he was okay with it finally. She kept her desires from her family until her brother came home from the army and could replace her in helping the family.

Sister Gabriella talked with wonder about how the "little ember" of her vocation was kept alive, how she tried, as she said, "on my side to pursue the one who pursued me." She remembered that she lit a candle before the Blessed Virgin for her vocation every Sunday after Mass, and how when she went to social events with friends, she felt that she didn't belong there. She said, "It is just like something else was pulling me in another direction, drawing me to another place."

She said that when she did enter, "I was just kind of taken over by grace." It was also a very different world; no one spoke Spanish and most of the other postulants had gone to school together at Catholic high schools. Sister Gabriella's technical-school education was not sufficient for her to be admitted to the University of Dallas with the others, so she and Sister Donna Marie audited classes there. Ironically, they are the only two of the eleven who entered together and remained sisters, except for Sister Paul, who is deceased. They entered in 1963, so she said they "ate up and breathed in and read everything about Vatican II."

During her second year as a novice, she was sent to Our Lady of Guadalupe parish in Wichita Falls because she could speak Spanish with the people of that neighborhood. She said, "First I was asked to forget Spanish, and then it was like 'these are your people.'" She was there for a year and found herself "getting back to my roots." She was still not prepared to get a higher education, so she educated herself in "more of a spiritual, theological, reflective way because obstacles placed in my way said it was against all odds. I truly believe that my natural abilities were enhanced by a loving God, by the power of the Holy Spirit that moves us and places us where we are to be, to the place where the heart begins to move in the direction that says 'but you can and you will, for I am here. I am the one who will be served by you.'"

Once again she attended college—this time at Texas Wesleyan—and while the others took classes for credit, she audited. One of the professors found out and challenged her to take the classes for credit, and her superior agreed that she could try it. Sister Gabriella said, "So, the first time I took the courses for credit, I got on the dean's list, and I never got off." She graduated cum laude, even though she was taking twenty-two hours in her last semesters.

Sister Gabriella said that she expanded her worldview when a group of young sisters about to make their perpetual vows were asked to go to Taizé to participate in the World Council of Youth. She said, "That is where I met sisters from England and Scotland and thousands of other people living in tents there for the council. I hadn't realized how many countries there were in the world and found the experience of being in such a large, international group 'incredible.'"

She started going to Mexico with Father Bob Thames and groups of young people. "We would go up to a village, and we would take a dentist, a medical doctor, an electrical engineer, and young adults who could dig and start construction for this or that clinic or some such project. We did that for several years." She said that this experience put her "in touch with the Mexican culture." Of course, they were very poor humble people in the villages who had very little or nothing.

After they had been going with the group for a few years, someone suggested that the sisters themselves go on their Christmas vacation and in the summers. Sister Gabriella reported, "A lot of young sisters participated. We took sewing machines; we had sewing classes up there; we took a little pharmacopoeia of all kinds of medications that were donated—vitamins, first aid kits, and OTC medications that could be administered. These small gestures turned out to also be a time with the women alone. You could hear their stories and pray with them."

After a while, the sisters began to work in more villages. The Benedictine priest from the monastery of Our Lady of Guadalupe in Morelia would drop the sisters off, celebrate Mass, and consecrate sufficient hosts to leave in the village church. The sisters prepared the children for First Holy Communion and led the village in rosaries, scripture, and talks—"all those kinds of things." Sister said that the community was so insular and isolated that this was "the only thing going on," and people would come from all over. She said, "They walked for hours to get there."

After graduation in the early 1970s, Sister Gabriella went to work in Wichita Falls again. It was a difficult time when many of the religious were leaving religious life. Sister Gabriella said, "It was like when somebody takes a rug from under your feet and people just start sliding off the floor. I lost a lot of my close friends, and that was a very deep pain for me because they invited me to go too." Sister Gabriella's response was, "It is not just about me but about the community and about ministry. My friends not only left religious life—some left the church. My point was 'What happens to the ministry? What happens to the people? What happens to the apostolate?' This covenant is not just with me and thee; it is about whole group of people." Sister Gabriella said that this was a difficult time. She had to "start again making new relationships." One of these relationships was with Sister Dorothy, who had been living in Morelia with the Guadalupana Sisters.

Sister Dorothy had been principal at Our Lady of Guadalupe, but she did not speak Spanish. She said the kids would say something and then laugh, and she did not like that she could not understand their language. Since she was still on the "summer plan" (that is, the sisters taught during the year and worked on their degree in the summers), she asked if she could go to Mexico and get her degree in Spanish. She completed the last two years of her degree at University of the Americas in Mexico City "all by myself and in secular clothes." At that time it was against the constitution in Mexico to wear the habit outside of the convent because of the principle of separation of church and state.

She began to go with the teams to rural Mexico. She said, "We would go up into the mountains, and it was a young person's ideal—no running water, no path, no toilet . . . just this house that was about the size of a bedroom, literally, where about six of us slept on the floor in bed rolls, just lined up like sardines. We would do catechesis, play games, and visit the people. I just loved it."

She said that three of them (Gabriella, Dorothy, and Kathy) began to talk about starting a foundation in Mexico. She said that since Gabriella was Mexican American, the superiors decided she didn't need any Mexican orientation, so she went to Rwanda for six months to see how the Sisters of St. Mary live a missionary life, while Kathy and Dorothy went to a formation program for missionaries going to Latin America.

Sister Gabriella and Sister Dorothy lived with a Mexican community in Morelia for two years (Sister Dorothy was there alone for six months while Sister Gabriella was in Rwanda; then they were there together for the last year and a half). She said they were trying to "learn the customs and culture and how things are done, and they were a missionary group, but they would do mobile teams to different towns and parishes that requested pastors. So we went on mission with them." Sister Gabriella said, "It was like on-the-job training in another country." She said that it was very helpful to them in learning the culture and the way things are done and also "in understanding which bishops would be more open to receiving American religious in their diocese. It was a very delicate type of work because some would say, 'Oh, sure. By the way, when you come, bring your SUV and bring this and that.' People don't understand that we don't have all these things."

After they received permission to begin, the Bishop of Acapulco took Sisters Gabriella and Dorothy way up in the middle of the country to an indigenous village. He said, "You know, people say 'Oh, Acapulco!' . . . but all of the money is right on the coast, and it is international—it comes in and it goes out. None of it helps the people here. A slight impediment to the situation, however, was that the Indians did not speak Spanish; they spoke their own language. It was too much to ask the sisters to learn two languages before starting a mission.

Later Mother Frances Elizabeth, the superior general who accompanied the sisters to Ciudad Altamirano, wisely said, "I don't know why we have to pick the hardest thing to do to start with," so they ended up on the coast, which was still twelve hours from Mexico City or from the diocesan seat.

Sister Gabriella said that the Mexican people treated her differently than they treated the other sisters. She said, "If a problem occurred, it was *'you* should know better.' I was supposed to remedy the problem. Any mistake in speech or custom was simply charming and amusing when the other sisters did it, but if I did it, it was a faux pas. I should know better. The pastor would take me aside and . . . he was not very affirming—let's put it that way."

The sisters went back to the United States, intending to stay only for a visit, but Sister Gabriella was asked to fill in with the new diocesan ministries program because Sister St. John had just been elected to the general council and Sister Dorothy needed surgery that required a long recovery. Since there was no one else to send, they had to close the mission. Sister Dorothy said, "It just broke my heart . . . it really did . . . I was just sobbing." Sister Gabriella said that it was a great loss. "It felt like having lost a child that one nurtures. You do all kinds of things to help make it grow and all of that . . . it just . . . it just was not to be."

Sister Gabriella and Sister Dorothy were able to use what they had learned to work with Spanish-speaking people in the new lay ministries program designed by Sisters Pat and Kay (School Sisters of Notre Dame). Sister Gabriella and Sister Dorothy were attending graduate school in the summers at St. Mary's University. Sister Gabriella reflected, "We were being formed as we were forming." Sisters Pat and Kay taught the English-speaking people and mentored Sister Gabriella and Sister Dorothy in what Sister Gabriella called "a wonderful way of teaching."

Next Sister Gabriella worked at the diocesan Hispanic office where she did "a bit of evangelization and a bit of everything." When people asked her about how to grow in their spiritual life, she felt that she needed more background and went to school to learn about it. She commented on her time in the Christian Spirituality Program at Creighton University: "You have to do a lot of journaling about what you are feeling and doing and all of that. So it became a way for me to really get underneath a lot of the layers." She said that she felt exhausted by the demands of her job: "running all over the diocese and collaborating with so many offices as the only Hispanic person, Spanish speaker, to do all of these different ministries that needed to be developed. I put a lot of pressure on myself trying to answer the demands." She also said that she met "many incredible people and wonderful friends" and that "the relationship made with these people is like a covenant that we have made to serve God."

She said that her experiences helped her to work with "the poor," and then she clarified that she was not just speaking of "the economically poor but also the intellectually poor, the people who haven't had a chance in life, the people who cannot articulate their needs. She wanted "to take time with them, to affirm them, to call them to give, to do, and to be." She said that she and Sister Dorothy had felt discouraged in the lay ministries program, thinking that they weren't seeing any results, until one day when they were at St. Mary's Church and they saw "the unity at St. Mary's—people helping at the Mass, doing all of the different ministries—they were all people that we had worked with." She said, "It is like giving birth. All that time, all that energy, believing that even a grandmother in the neighborhood can have a prayer group in her home and that she knows the dynamics and how to lead and how to share, breaking open the Word of God . . . clearly it is not just about doing but of being the type of person who sees the dignity of the other and does not put them down because of the way they talk or the way they are or because of whatever prejudices we carry." Sister Gabriella said, "I think all of my upbringing has led me to this moment." She saw how her experience of how people told her she couldn't do this or she couldn't be that helped prepare her for ministry. She said "Well, by God, we are certainly going to try; we're going to try to do whatever it takes to take our place; we're going to try to be part of this church, and we are going to try to take our place along with everybody else."

In 2000 Sister Gabriella was asked to work with the international novitiate, where everyone was from a different country. "We had several different languages. There were young sisters from Dominican Republic, Canada, Cameroon, Scotland, and Brazil." The novitiate was for sisters in countries that did not have enough novices to have their own novitiate. Once again Sister Gabriella encountered a language challenge: the novitiate was in Belgium where the sisters were to speak French. She said that she could speak Spanish to the Brazilians and to the sister from the Dominican Republic. Again her experience in lay ministry helped her to believe that they could do it. She said that someone said that they were all just going to have to speak French. When asked in French "What language are we going to speak here?" the sisters were to respond "French." When Gabriella was asked, she responded with the French phrase that means "the language of the novitiate is charity." She said that she said what she did because of her experience with "the alienation that occurs when you don't speak your own language; this is a negation of what a person is at one's core, an alienation of 'heart-terms' where one expresses the deeper realities in one's life." Gabriella explained further,

> For example, I cannot talk about falling in love with God in an unfamiliar language. I have to hear God speak in my own language, in the language of my heart, and allow it to penetrate into my own being and allow the words to resonate in my heart with their full emotional impact so that I can savor and say "yes" to that love. The God conversation relates to what in the end is most intimate within the person. We need to find the language that expresses this reality for us, whatever that language happens to be, because it will determine who I am and what I believe. Falling in love with God determines if I will get up in the morning; it is why I am moved do all these things I am called to do. Therefore, it is necessary to continue to remember and cherish our call, to listen again to the language of love, of the first love, of what or who it was that drew you. What attracted you? What moved you? What or who captured your heart? What gift do I give in return?

> It is a combination of all these elements that coalesce in the mind, the heart, and the spirit of the person, which are not simply elusive sentiments or feelings but . . . have to do with direction, decision, choice, commitment, and response. It is a choice to continue to grow, to continue to deepen, to allow oneself to be nourished, to open the gift. It is so easy to be turned around in our culture. There are so many things that can attract you or distract you from the one thing necessary. People, things, and places. And yet ultimately it is about that underlying relationship with God. I believe that just as in a marriage a couple's love can bring about a birth, so too I have to ask myself "How am I being fruitful? What are you bringing to birth?"

Sister Gabriella later served on the general council and visited houses in other countries. She said that she was touched when she visited Rwanda to see that every house is involved in ministries, but "one person in the house has a ministry to the vulnerable." She said, "I went to a camp where they have a place named the House of Mercy where there is a group of people who are suffering from AIDS and they are all just very, very debilitated. Oh! You could tell they had been quite ill and were so fragile, their eyes were red. They were shelling peanuts, and a sister said, 'Oh, they are working right now.' Even the feeblest person who is almost unable to do anything has a job to do." She said that it is part of their dignity to be able to contribute in this way. This house also has people with AIDS but who are in recovery; they come to visit and share with the residents to mentor them towards life.

The sister there said that there are many orphans of the men and women who have died, and each house has an outreach. She added,

> I use the word the way we use it here . . . but it is much more intimate; it is much more personal with the people who are touched by AIDS. This is to me the most exciting part—to see how God works in this area with women, our sisters, who have lost so many family members, women who are deeply grieved and who continue to grieve, who will never be the

same, who have been touched by the hand of evil in the loss of so many of their family members, who have lost them to the genocide. Where death abided, life is now exploding; mercy is unbounded. There was a sister, who had worked up in the refugee camps, and she was telling me how the various charitable organizations bring in the food and supplies to give to families, but she said, "You know, they don't give it to the widows. They don't give it to the children. They don't give it to the elderly. You have to get in there and get it; you have to be proactive for the poor."

So, the sister continued,

I went and I stayed and I stayed and I stayed and begged and begged until they gave me food, and then I was able to say, "Here, Mama, this is for you." One must be proactive for life. What happens to the person who lives in our midst who is literally starving, who is dying, or who is sickly? How do we take care of them? How do we reach them? How does their suffering touch us and move us to some action on their behalf? That same sister was showing me her pictures of the refugee camp, and then she suddenly came upon another group of pictures, and it was the picture of a skeleton laid out on the ground on a straw mat. She picked it up and said, "This is my sister. Do you see her teeth? This is her; this is her skeleton." She pointed at it and said, "This is her. When I came back from Congo, all of my family had disappeared. She [the skeleton in the picture] is the only one I have found." The sister went back to the village where her family lived and by asking questions was able to find her sister. "We went back to our hill, and we went up the hill. I asked different people, and then I came upon this cloth that had been her dress." The sister didn't say it with rancor; she didn't say it with bitterness. She said it with joy that she had found one member of her family. She said, "Then I went to the radio station because I thought there may be some other people around, like my family." So she made an announcement on Radio Rwanda, and a cousin from Tanzania heard it and came to see her. I don't know any of the sisters in that area who didn't suffer grievous loss. To me, it's like the scripture says, "Behold, this is a mystery." You see nothing but death and darkness and evil, but moving out and away from that place, you now see these sisters reborn by grace and the Spirit. This is now our spiritual relationship and bonding. Darkness has given way to light. Born out of the terrible suffering, our congregation has been enriched through grace. Through this event we have experienced the paschal mystery. The world very easily forgets, but we who remember can seize the costly grace brushing so close to us.

Chapter 4

Free Will Was God's Idea, Not Mine[1]

RELIGIOUS LIFE prior to the late 1950s and 1960s was "vacuum packed, preserved from eras before them, a fossil of ages past," according to Sister Joan Chittister, a Benedictine.[2] She said, "For the average Catholic, Vatican II was a new way of thinking about church, faith, and the world. For women religious, however, Vatican II meant a whole new way of living, of relating, of being in the world."[3] Mary Luke Tobin, a Loretto sister who was present at Vatican II, said, "Something new was happening. A door marked 'change' was quietly opening to a much wider vision of the church and of religious life. Even as it invited us across the threshold, it intimated an uncompromising unequivocal demand for wide-ranging and painful readjustments."[4]

Change is not easy for most people, and change that reaches to the very root of one's life and soul is breathtakingly difficult. Change for the Sisters of St. Mary, like other religious sisters, was further complicated by the fact that they experienced it differently depending upon their age, their theology, and their personalities. When people dress alike and have the same structures for prayer

---

1. The title of this chapter is a quote from Sister Mary Patricia, who went through much of the Vatican II aftermath.
2. Chittister, *The Way We Were*, 207.
3. Chittister, *The Way We Were*, 71.
4. Tobin, "Women in the Church," 295–96.

and community life, it is easy to assume that they think alike. One of the painful aspects of this period of time was that they discovered that people held very different views. It is as if when the habit came off the people under it were exposed in all their uniqueness.

This was a difficult time for the sisters to live and to talk about; however, I think they have valuable lessons to teach us about learning to live well with people who see things very differently than we do. Their stories are lessons for us all and perhaps more important in today's world than ever before. There are some golden threads that shine through this era. Sisters repeatedly said that it was their love for each other that allowed them to move through the difficulties and that it was their commitment to God and to serving people that required them to be true to their vision of what that meant and how it should be lived. While most of them would like to have not gone through the difficult times, they believe it was worthwhile and that they have grown because of it.

Difficult as the times were for the sisters, they were even more difficult for the three women who were the superiors during these years. Sister Alice Claire was there at the beginning and was so upset that she asked to be relieved of the last year of her term. She was known to be a "beautiful woman" but with a kind of rigidity that made it very difficult to take risks. Sister St. John said that Sister Alice Claire had said that the renewal was "not a passing thing. It was at the heart of our understanding of God and how we live our lives and how we pass it on. We could not afford to make a mistake." When one feels that kind of responsibility and does not have the freedom to make mistakes, it is very difficult to lead people through the kind of changes that characterized those times.

Sister Mary Patricia replaced Sister Alice Claire and led the Texas SSMNs during the next difficult nine years. Many of the sisters described her as "our prophet" and "visionary." There was not a sister in SSMN who was not touched by her. One of the former sisters said that Sister Mary Patricia was "a very special friend. I bet you've talked to seventy-five people who say she was a very special friend. Each one of us feels that way." Sister Mary Patricia said she was there "for eternity." It may have seemed that way as she attempted to guide the community through a very difficult nine years.

SISTER MARY PATRICIA

Sister Mary Patricia entered SSMN in 1939. She described it as an easy decision. She said, "I never thought much about it. Everybody knew I was going to be a sister before I did. I just heard these things from these priests, saying I know not what . . . but it just made me realize that that's what I wanted to do. No great revelation. I'm almost convinced that you live with people and you like what you see and you want to do that."

Once she was there, it wasn't all that easy. She talked about many days when she began walking toward her parents' house with the intention of leaving. She said,

> I just lived across the street. Several times I was going home. I got to about half of the yard over there and would come back. I would get very angry at the sister in charge of the novices. I just didn't see much sense in a lot of stuff, but I just did it. I've always felt that that was a great advantage in the people in my time. You knew things didn't make a lot of sense, but if they didn't make a lot of sense, don't make a big fuss about them. . . . when people had such a hard time with rules and things like that, I could never understand why they would be so upset; just do it and get it over with.

Sister Mary Patricia had a lifelong struggle with anger and was known for saving burned-out light bulbs to throw against the brick wall of the incinerator or repeatedly pulling the wooden blinds all the way to the top of a large window and letting them fall. Her experience with her own anger came in handy later when she was superior. She said that when a sister came in really angry at one of the other sisters, she would hand her some of the little ceramic nun dolls that were popular at the time and suggest the sister go throw them against the incinerator wall.

Perhaps part of what allowed Sister Mary Patricia to be the kind of superior who could knit together a community of great diversity was that she grew up with parents whose view of the church was different from each other in the extreme. She said, "My father thought the church could do nothing wrong and my mother thought the church could do nothing right." Many sisters said that it was easy to talk with Sister Mary Patricia and that her responses were sensible and wise. She seemed to be an interesting combination of deep understanding and practicality, and she was not afraid of other sisters' anger even when they were angry with God. Many said that they aspired to be like her or that she had a special connection with them, and then they added "everybody has the same kind of special connection with her and would like to be like her."

EXPERIMENTATION

Sister Mary Luke Tobin noted, "Even before the Vatican Council, fresh insights into the church as community, openness to new directions in biblical studies, a more participatory liturgy, and a developing ecumenical movement were appearing. A sense of the importance of social justice and its interdependence with these new movements was finding its way into the lives of women religious, and religious communities began to incorporate some of these ideas. This sense of a changing climate was perceptibly increasing in the 1950s and early 1960s."

Before Vatican II was convened the sisters began to get "little snippets of news" in anticipation of the decisions of the council. Some priests offered Mass facing the people, there was a little more freedom, and the sisters began introducing students to scriptures in a way that was easier to understand. They read the readings in English and began using music other than what Sister Jane called "that insipid St. Basil hymnal."

Where freedom wasn't given, it was sometimes taken. Sister Josephine reported, "I had already taken off the habit and everything without any kind of permission. I just thought it was time to do it. So I went out and bought several outfits and came back to St. James. I was the superior and I said, 'Everybody can take so-and-so amount of money and go and buy some clothes,' and we just did it."

Experimental communities for the Sisters of St. Mary of Namur in the missions meant, as we saw in Sister Rosemary's story, living among the people they served, cooking over wood fires, and carrying water from its source. In the United States it took a variety of forms. Some sisters lived in small groups in houses, and some intentionally lived among the poor people they served. Sister Patricia Ridgley was living with young sisters in early vows who said that Vatican II had said they should go back to their origins. They said, "If our origins are with the poor of Namur, how come we're living in these convents?" She said that the superior, Sister Mary Patricia, told them to "give it a try." Sister Patricia said, "So we rented this little house, this little shotgun house. We were all stuffed into that house—there were probably three or four of us and sharing little spaces with a little space for our chapel. We had our prayers, and they were still going to college, and I would go to work. We were getting to know our neighbors. . . . it was just a different kind of experience altogether." She added, "Those were fine young women, you know, really asking hard questions lots of times and big questions."

The difficulties created by so much freedom highlighted differences in the community, and there were disagreements, discussions, and an evolution of understanding. Former sister Mary Mc. said,

> There were different opinions about community life, both in the structure of it and how we were to live it. There were even different opinions about prayer together . . . this way or that way and, of course, the habit. We began to realize that different ones of us have a different theology of religious life. It stayed under cover while we were all living it. But when

everything was exposed, it became more obvious and we went through some difficult times. We weren't accepting of each other's theology or each other's desire to live this way or to dress this way. We were constantly calling one another to acceptance and to respect, but it was a struggle. Whether you were more conservative or more liberal, we all had to learn how to live with and to respect each one.

Because it was a theology, it was coming from our soul, and from our prayer life and from our theology of religious life, and it was not superficial. It was coming from way down deep. It was extremely important to us to have the dialogue, even when the person you were dialoguing with seemed to have a wall up. With time we shed our defenses and we began to accept each other. Exterior things such as the habit, my gosh, we don't even think about that. But in the early days, that was problematic.

THE NIGHT THEY DROVE OL' DIXIE DOWN

The changes were not implemented uniformly in all parts of the SSMN. The sisters in Texas had changed more rapidly than other provinces. Six of the Texas sisters were delegates to the General Chapter in Belgium in 1971. One of the sisters said that they had documented everything, written their requests to Belgium, and "everything that had been proposed at Texas was refused." Another sister reported that the voting on almost all of the issues was thirty to six. Sister Josephine said, "We were afraid to come home because we had been doing all of this experimentation; we had come with all these proposals, and none of them had gone through, and so we were afraid to come home and report." In a dramatic metaphor for the times, they said that the six delegates left in street clothes and came home in habits.

Sister Josephine said that to avoid going back to Texas immediately, the six

> took off in a Buick Opal and double tent that we had to put up every night when we went camping from Namur, Belgium, all

the way down to Taizé, France, and back. The first night it was getting toward dusk, and we saw a farmer's field, and so we asked him if we could put up our tent. We had not practiced putting up this heavy, heavy tent. It had two roofs on it so you had to coordinate putting both of them up at the same time with this middle pole and then driving the stakes in, etc. We asked Sister Mary Patricia to stand in the middle and hold the pole. It collapsed on top of her, and it was just this huge tent ... with this little mound in the middle and Sister Mary Patricia saying, "Help! Help! I can't breathe!" We were laughing and she said, "Stop laughing and get me out of here."

Former sister Mary said that when they came home and gave the report at a meeting, "tears started coming down." She added, "I recall how crowded that little front room was. It seemed dark, possibly because we had so many people in there that they were blocking the windows. People were crying and yelling." She said that it was during that chapter that she had "the final break with—in my own heart—the international community. I didn't realize it until I got in the car and burst into tears. I sobbed all the way back to the east side of Fort Worth, where I was living. I had never experienced anything like that. It was like I was dying. That was the break at the time." She said that break was only with the international community, not with the sisters of this province, and "the proof of that is that it took me thirteen years to finally leave the community."

Sister Mary Merdian, who was superior after Sister Mary Patricia, recalled that night:

> At that time we had a different superior general, and she was really very strong and unyielding. I remember when they came back from that meeting. Those of us who had been doing experimentations, who were out of the habit and so on, were called to a meeting, and I remember Sister Jane Conway had learned the song "The Night They Drove Old Dixie Down," and she kept playing it and we kept singing it. Poor Sister Mary Patricia was in tears the whole evening. I think we were beginning to see that it was a matter of relationships, of going out to really minister to the people we were with. At that time I had gone out of the habit, and we were doing

> experimenting at our house. We were told it had to stop, that we were supposed to put the veil back on and so on. Mary Patricia never really enforced that; she took a very large view of that rule. The relations we had with the people were so different. We would take the kids camping on weekends and have overnights with the kids. Their parents related so well; we had the sense that we could really bring God to the people. That was the struggle; it wasn't just about externals. There was a lot of difficulty about the habit within the community, and it took a long time to pass. I think it was the love we had for one another and for God that got us through that.

Sister Josephine said that the congregation as a whole was not ready for what the Texas province was doing, so the Texas novitiate was closed in 1968, and the women who entered had to go to Buffalo and be part of that novitiate. Sister Donna Ferguson and Sister Rosemary were novices at the time and, with little notice, they were sent to the novitiate in New York. Sister Rosemary said, "When we were in the novitiate in New York, we had to decide if we were going to remain part of the Buffalo province. The general superior said that if we wanted to go back to Texas, "you have to prolong your novitiate another year to live in that province for a while before you decide if you want to ask to make profession."

EXODUS

Some sisters still speak with nostalgia about the days when a large chapel was filled with row upon row of habited sisters. The old ways for some are so associated with the times before their numbers diminished that they are inseparable in their minds. Sister Joan Chittister said that this was true in her community, even though there were more women entering and more women leaving just before the changes associated with Vatican II. It is impossible to know how much of the exodus was due to the renewal of religious life and how much was due to broader cultural changes that, among other things, created more opportunities for women. In any case, the loss of sisters was, and is, painful for those who remained.

Some of the sisters who stayed lost sisters they had gone through novitiate with and, in many cases, people they had been in school with, sometimes since elementary school. Older sisters had known those who left because they had taught them or directed them in novitiate. It was a painful time for all of them.

Sister St. John said that a lot of the sisters left the community after they received their education at the University of Dallas. Sister explained it this way: "If you entered to give your life to God, then everything else is incidental, and that's what I think it's about. But if you entered mainly because you saw people doing what you would like to do, you pretty soon found out that you could do that without being a sister. So we got a lot of people trained and most of them are out there doing beautiful things. Many of them are working in parishes or all sorts of things."

Sister St. John said,

> It was very hard for me personally because I had directed them as "juniors." That was my job and I had known them personally, so it was really hard. But then when I was making a retreat, just before I came home after my six years in Belgium, I began to be haunted by sister this and sister that and I began just writing them down. There was a long list of them. They were beautiful, talented, competent people we had counted on for our future, and they were gone. So I just kept writing them down and decided if I wanted to sleep at night, I was going to have to do something about this. So, I got the whole list, found the statue of the Blessed Mother and said, "You take care of them!"

Sister St. John said "they are doing God's work where they are and they're following their call as they see it." I asked Sister if there were any women who left that she believed had been called to give their life to God as a member of this community. She said "yes" and then, characteristically added, "And then I realized, that wasn't my call." She said that she just had "to trust that they had done in the first place what they thought God wanted and that they were doing in the second place what they thought God wanted."

Sister Jane said that having so many sisters leave "was definitely hard for our community. It can be hard for a religious community to contain the great thinkers, and I'm not saying all were—some were. They were all very well educated, pretty much across the board, and they were articulate. Some have gotten married; they've gone on very definite different tracks in their life. But some have not. I wish it all had not happened."

Sister Ann Vincent said,

> That was sad at that time when we had so many walk out. Actually those people would be the people who are to be in authority now, to be the government now. That's what we're feeling, that's the crunch. It was also growth for us. We were never too many, but we were not that close, although we wanted to be. There were many among us who were so silenced that they couldn't express themselves, which was a bad thing for us too. The young group, the new generation, they are very vocal. It was difficult, but we just had to live it, and that was hard.

In the early days, the sisters who stayed could not have any contact with a sister who left without express permission from the superior, and often the sisters didn't know a sister was leaving until she was gone. Sister Ann Vincent recalled driving the provincial and another sister to Wichita Falls. When they arrived, she saw that the sister had a suitcase, and that was the first inkling she had that the sister was leaving.

A former sister, Linda, said "Now that I'm older and look back on it, I can understand that the older sisters were having a little bit of a panic attack because it was as if we all thought the world would be different in a year or so just because of the renewal coming through Vatican II. Those with more life experience viewed that facile perspective with some skepticism . . . and rightly so." She added, "The other thing that happened in the dynamics of the community discussion (and this may seem to contradict what I just said) . . . the group that was five to seven years older than those of us in our early- and mid-twenties had completed their professional formation. They would explore with us cutting-edge ideas and thought concerning change in the church and the world. And we got into defending 'the truth' which sometimes was the 'status quo'; for a time that was our youthful form of rebellion. Finally our life experience matured us, and we became more open."

Sister Josephine believes that a lot of the people who left did so because they felt they were being asked to go backwards, that the congregation was not going to change quickly enough. She said,

> Who knows the difference between me and those who left? I really believe that we went through a very dark and difficult period. It's a psychological thing; it's really not a spiritual or religious thing. It was more a matter of who could endure. My best friends left. I remember thinking that I have lived through all the craziness and I don't think God is going to give up on us. But we had to laugh about it and we had to joke about it. You've got to be able to do that and at the same time know that being obedient to God doesn't necessarily mean being obedient to what those people in the General Chapter said. It was a process. And it did get better within the next ten years.

The charismatic renewal of the church was also going on at the same time as all of these changes. Some SSMN sisters were very active in charismatic communities, particularly in Wichita Falls, Texas. Sister Ginny said that a sister who was regional superior left with five charismatic sisters to begin a charismatic community and asked Sister Ginny and Sister Patricia Ste. Marie to go too. Sister Ginny said "She wanted to be free of the institution, and she said we were in bondage to the institution." Sister Ginny and Sister Patricia Ste. Marie decided that they did not agree with that, and they decided to stay. They did feel for a while that they were in a bit of a precarious position, however. Sister Ginny said that when the general superior made a visitation, she found them living in a charismatic community, and Sister Ginny seemed to think from the general superior's comments that being asked to leave was a real possibility, but they decided not to leave unless they were told to leave. Sister Ginny said, "That just freed us. We said, 'we're not going anywhere, and if you don't like this, you're going to have to tell us to leave." But then the general superior would keep questioning us and, finally, when we thought we were going to be booted out, they asked Patricia to be in charge of formation and me to be assistant."

Sister Mary Merdian was provincial after Sister Mary Patricia. She said that the ones who left who talked with her seemed to really pray and discern about leaving and that it was not an easy decision for them. She said,

> I think once we began to experience more outward communication with people and new ministries began to open up, there was such internal conflict; it opened up something within all of us in searching for what was our next step. How do we move into the future? I think Vatican II opened us to some realities, and I think that was at the source of a lot of the leaving. I think at the time they entered, it was the only thing a woman could do to serve the church. Some of them saw new possibilities; some were attracted to things they had never experienced. Most of us that were in at that time had entered when we were seventeen, right out of high school. I feel that their motivation was very sincere, very well thought through, and that they really searched what God was calling them to. I find it very interesting that so many of these women have never married and continued the same type of ministry they were already in. There were some that left with bitterness, and that was difficult, but most of them left with a good feeling and a good relationship.

HEALING

Right before she left office, Sister Mary Patricia hired MDI, a consultation firm, to work with the province. That process began under Sister Mary Merdian, when she succeeded Sister Mary Patricia as provincial. Sister Mary Merdian called those times "terrible years" and times of "a lot of heartache and pain and searching." She said it was painful because they were seriously considering breaking away from the general congregation and there were vast differences among the sisters about this. She said, "The picture I have in my mind the most about that whole time was one day when we had to physically get up and if we were for pulling away get on one side of the room and if we were against it get on the other. We stood there looking at each other. There was such love. . . . there has always been such love among the sisters. . . . I think that was so painful for us."

She said,

> At first I think there was a little bit of reaction to MDI coming because a lot of the sisters saw it as someone trying to tell us what to do, whereas their job was really facilitation. We continued with an individual from the company, with Sister Deanna, and with another sister that she teamed with to help us through the discernment period. I think we grew a lot during that time of MDI and during the time of our discernment. I think we learned how to listen to each other on a much deeper level and try to understand what others were seeing that we did not understand.

She said that MDI helped them to write what she called "a value-oriented budget," that is, to review the budget to see if it reflected the values of the congregation. She said that it "was a very good point of view to think about—were we living what we profess to live and did that show in our budget?" As if that were not enough, the international congregation as a whole was writing the constitutions at that time, which meant that there were extra meetings and "there was always a lot of struggle about what Texas wanted to do and why, why couldn't we put this into the constitution, and why do we have to leave that in and so on."

Shortly before Sister Mary Merdian became provincial, a new general superior of the congregation was elected. The new superior had definite ideas about religious life, but she also was interested in finding a solution to the problems in Texas and the exodus of sisters. The sisters began a one-year "discernment group" that was made up of anyone who wanted to be a part of it, about thirty to thirty-five sisters. The group, called "the study group," met monthly for a year with Sister Ruby (one of the MDI consultants) facilitating the process. Sister Ruby's congregation had been through a similar process of discerning whether to stay with their original affiliation or break off and affiliate with the diocese. By the end of the year, "it evolved" that the Texas province stayed with the international SSMN. Sister Mary said that they still lost a few sisters, but not nearly as many as they had prior to these discussions.

Much later at a general chapter, the congregation thanked the Texas sisters for leading them into the future. Specifically, the congregation was grateful to Texas for new ideas they brought about leadership and facilitation, for the Texas stance on non-violence,[5] and the work of Sister Anselma and others on the Justice and Peace Committee, and for new ways of being a part of the congregation in the form of oblates and associates.[6] Sister Mary Merdian described this as "the resurrection moment," following the cross of the difficult times that preceded it.

Sister Theresa said, "I really couldn't understand why, because I didn't feel the way they did. I thought 'God, why am I in with these people, and none of us see things the same way?' I think what I was really thinking was, 'none of them see things the way I do.'" She said it was particularly vivid when the consultants had them move to sides of the room based on whether they thought they should break from the general congregation and Sister Teresa was surprised to find that some of her closest friends were on the opposite side of the room. She said, "I thought 'How could this be?'" She added,

> We've stayed friends with those who left, and I think the ones who stayed have become much closer. Possibly it's from having gone through that, I don't know. I think we were able to accept the fact that it wasn't something personal about us that caused the others to leave. It was just a difference in how we saw our relationship with God and with one another, and we really didn't all have to think exactly alike. I think that was

---

5. The SSMN as a whole later adopted a similar stance against violence in all of its forms.

6. These new forms of membership are described in the next chapter.

a big revelation for a lot of us. For that reason I was glad we went through that. But I sure was glad it was over. We finally could accept the fact that everybody who had thought that they had been called to this life hadn't really been, and once they discovered this, they had no choice but to go. We could all stay friends, and many of those former sisters come back and visit. Those who left still have a lot of the spirit of the community and have close relationships within the community.

Some of the former sisters do more than visit, like the former sister who is an attorney (and a judge) who continues to handle the sisters' legal matters.

Sister Teresa continued,

> I'm beginning to see what people mean when they say they may have been called to this life for a time, to fulfill a certain end that God had, and then they're called to go in a different direction. For a while, I thought "No, once God has called you, that's it." But God can change his call. They were being true to what *they* were hearing God say, not necessarily what *we* thought God was saying. It's a conflict within the person themselves that they have to resolve, and they have to resolve it their way, according to their personalities, their knowledge of God, their relationship with God, and so on. I think it's true of the events in our lives that at the time we go through them, it's a real conflict and it's very, very difficult to see how it's all blending. It's not until we get past it and can look back that it makes sense. I've heard it compared to a weaving. When the weaver sees it as they're working it, everything is all. . . strings going every which way and it doesn't look like it's a pattern. Then when they see it from the front, it's a beautiful pattern. I think that's the way it is with the events in our lives; at the time we don't know where it's going, we don't understand how it's fitting together.

One of the things that helped heal the rupture between the sisters who left and those who stayed was a program designed by Sister Josephine. Sister Josephine had designed "Beginning Experience" for divorced, widowed, and separated people as well as their children, so she had professional expertise in helping people recover from loss. She said that she designed "a program of closure for our former sisters and the community. We had a marvelous, marvelous retreat based on going through the grief process."

Sister Ann Vincent said of the first gathering, "It was sad, but it was good. They got in there and they just aired everything. They just talked about it. That was the conversion, or the getting together again, and after that the sisters here went out of their way to be there for those people and to include them and to do things. . . . there was a bending on both sides that was absolutely necessary."

Sister Mary Patricia was at the first meeting and she continued to support the effort by meeting with a group that was called "the support group" formed out of this first meeting. Sister Louise said, "At one time we weren't supposed to have any connection to anybody who left. I credit Sister Mary Patricia, I think, with that change because as I say, she was an extraordinary woman open to all kinds of ideas. You knew where she stood on principles, but she was always willing to listen. And if she saw that she was wrong or maybe too rigid on something, she was always ready to admit it. Now she wasn't wishy-washy. But she was willing to change if the change was the right thing to do." Sister Louise said that she thought that Sister Mary Patricia realized that to fail to maintain relationship with the sisters who left was "really very uncharitable."

I think we have much to learn from the sisters and their hard-won experience of community. As Ronald Rolheiser said, "To be in apostolic community, church, is not necessarily to be with others with whom we are emotionally, ideologically, and otherwise compatible. Rather, it is to stand, shoulder to shoulder and hand in hand, precisely with people who are very different from ourselves and, with them, hear a common word, say a common creed, share a common bread, and offer mutual forgiveness so as, in that way, to bridge our differences and become a common heart."[7]

---

7. Rolheiser, *The Holy Longing*, 115.

Free Will Was God's Idea, Not Mine

SOCIAL JUSTICE: SISTER PATRICIA RIDGLEY AND FORMER SISTER LINDA

Part of Vatican II's call for the renewal of religious life was a call to renewed commitment to the community's original purpose. The Sisters of St. Mary of Namur originated in a call to social justice and a preferential option for the poor. The sisters have been involved in peace and justice movements since their beginning, but their work intensified during this period. Sister Mary Patricia said that a renewed sensitivity to social justice issues was one of the gifts brought to the community by the younger sisters. Former sister Linda and Sister Patricia Ridgley provided me with some insight into this gift.

Sister Patricia Ridgley said that her sensitivity to issues of justice began when she was chosen along with another sister to go to Belgium after her postulant year. At the age of nineteen, she had lived her whole life in Dallas, Texas, and she felt that she entered another world. She said, "I'll always remember that. There were probably thirty other young women, including some of our first novices from Rwanda and Congo. I still remember being in awe that there were African sisters, Belgian sisters, and English sisters." She saw her own racism when she realized with a jolt, "I'm going to be living with people of color." Sister Patricia had gone to a mostly European American school with few girls of color and no African Americans. She said her first awareness of the commonality between the sisters from Texas and the sisters from Africa was during the long, cold, dark winters of Belgium—when the sun came out, the sisters from Texas and Africa were all out in the yard. She said, "We had that in common; we were from places of sun and light."

After she returned and finished her degree, Sister Patricia taught high school. She was teaching about the documents of Vatican II and especially the Catholic social justice teaching. She said "Little by little in the course of teaching my students about those documents, I started understanding the roots of justice and poverty."

THE ARMS OF GOD

The civil rights movement was taking hold in these times, and the Southern Christian Leadership Conference (SCLC) had started a group in Dallas. Sister Patricia and an African American sister began going to SCLC meetings on Saturday mornings. Sister Patricia said it

> brought together all these folks from the neighborhood. There was preaching first of all, singing, and then strategizing what were the issues we should be working on. . . . The preaching started connecting the gospel and the concrete justice in the street, for me, in a way that the University of Dallas had not done and, of course, couldn't have done. Week after week, they had this extraordinary young Baptist minister who had worked with Dr. King, Peter Thompson, who was the heart of the beginning of the Southern Leadership Conference in Dallas. Kathy and I would come back and say, "Gosh, it was just inspiring and challenging." Then you had to say, "Well, what does that mean? What do we do?"
>
> I started understanding my own city in a different way. Going to the meetings of the SCLC, I was driving through areas I have never driven through as a white kid growing up in Dallas. I started seeing the structures of my city and a lot of things about my own town that I hadn't realized. One of the things I started understanding was that one of the reasons Africa was so poor was because of the banking system in Dallas, Texas. I started seeing those kinds of connections and realized maybe that's what needs to be worked on if I really want to be part of changing and helping Africa.

Until that time Sister Patricia had hoped to return to Africa, where she had lived for a time. She said that after she came to the realization that there was work to be done here, she stopped requesting to return to Africa.

> Part of working with SCLC was moving beyond theoretically thinking about justice and peace to taking action and being part. . . . I remember the first time we were part of the picket line at a grocery store in Dallas in an inner-city neighborhood. Blacks were only employed as janitors . . . and yet all the customers were African American. All the clerks and people

Free Will Was God's Idea, Not Mine

working the registers were white, and they banked in white banks across town. We did all of this analysis in the Saturday morning meeting; you're really putting gospel and economics right here, and so we participated with some other groups and picketing. That was the first time I'd ever done anything like that. Sister Mary Patricia was our provincial at the time. Kathy and I called her and said, "We're going to do this." I still remember, because it was going to rankle the establishment of the community, the great Catholic people who probably owned the grocery store, so . . . we called Sister Mary Patricia. I remember Sister Mary Patricia said, "Now look here, if you girls get arrested, just make sure it's for something worthwhile." That was the counsel. She got a lot of irate phone calls. Kathy and I were photographed holding a vigil, still in a habit, along with all the other people. That was hard . . . when you move from believing something to doing something uncomfortable, not knowing what it's going to do. Having once done that, then there's a freedom that you kind of move into, a different way of feeling, a different way of understanding what might need to be done. Again, the Sisters of St. Mary supported us. That's a different story than what a lot of people had to deal with; they had a lot more resistance. I'll never know whether the people in our community found this offensive. Sister Mary Patricia dealt with those people. She never talked about that.

In 1972 or so, Sister Mary Patricia said that since they had taught "decades in Oak Cliff," it was time to work with the families of the children too. She asked Sister Patricia to begin doing pastoral work at Holy Cross Church, a mostly African American parish. She said,

> I began working there at Holy Cross as a pastoral associate. I didn't know what in the world the word meant or what we were going to do." The pastor said, "I think the first thing I would do is just go house to house and visit with parishioners." So I did that, and it was a really great way to get to know the parishioners. The parish was in the process, when I came in those early years, of moving from largely white, Czech farmers who had built the parish in 1956. Bishop College was an African American college that moved into the neighborhood in the 1970s or the late 1960s and caused the classic white

flight in this whole area. There was a real change of people in the parish that was happening, so we spent a lot of the early years helping to build the new leadership, helping smooth over old leadership, helping to keep the old parishioners and to welcome the new parishioners, as it was moving from largely white to an almost all African American parish. Pastoral work with Father Tim was a really marvelous way to begin to understand because he had no boundaries. If you are in Dallas working for the poor or working with issues for the families and you cross a parish boundary, it didn't matter to him. It was like the world is my parish, and he had a great sense of that.

Former sister Linda said that she was living in the house where Sister Patricia lived and that Father Tim would often join them for supper in the evenings. She said that she mentioned to him casually one evening at dinner that she would like to get into parish work. She said that later he asked if she would be interested in becoming campus minister at Bishop College, which was a black college. She said that the community agreed, and she not only did campus ministry with the Bishop College students but also youth ministry with the parish. She said that community colleges weren't as common as they are now, so she "did young adult ministry where I tried to get the Bishop College kids together with our young adults who were not able to go college because they intellectually didn't have the background or because they couldn't afford it."

Linda and Sister Patricia were part of the protest at the Comanche Peak nuclear power plant, which resulted in Sister Patricia being arrested (the charges were later dropped). As part of their peace efforts, the community had met Sister Rosalee, a sister from the Northeast who "had done all her academic work on the effects of low level radiation. So they called Sister Rosalee Burtelle, whom we had never met before, down to do some expert witness stuff for the trial for Patricia and another person, whose civil disobedience in connection with the protest had led to her arrest."

Free Will Was God's Idea, Not Mine

Years later, Sister Patricia had cancer and was being treated for it, and Linda had been in Europe working with peace groups. They had two Maryknoll sisters living with them and on December 2, 1980, four American churchwomen were killed in El Salvador, including Maryknoll Sisters Maura Clarke and Ita Ford. The sister who lived with them knew one of the sisters who had been killed. Sister Patricia said that the inspiration of the women who were killed was one of the things that helped her move past the soul-searching about religious life. She said, "We were already working on Central American issues, and Bishop Romero had been assassinated earlier that year, and out of that was all of the liberation theology and religious reflection on the struggle that was touching me very much. I think that was my confirmation that religious life can be of significance in the world of war and poverty—that there can be meaning in that."

Linda said,

> Even though Patricia was still doing pretty heavy duty chemo, all of us managed to get together a really wonderful ecumenical service citywide. I mean 200 people, which in Dallas is extraordinary. It's like five thousand in New York City, you know. I remember standing in the back of the church looking at all of these people, most of whom I knew. So you had women religious; you had a lot of church people: Methodist, Lutherans, Catholics. And then we had all of these atheists there from these different political parties—I don't know how Patricia and I got to know them—but anyway, there were a lot of different people. Like there was a guy there passing out the *Daily Worker*.

She said that they then "started the religious task force on Central America and the Committee on Solidarity with People of El Salvador." Linda was coordinator of the community-based task force, and Sister Patricia coordinated the church-based one. Sister Patricia said,

> In the 1980s our community, along with the parish we were in, came through a discernment process with the parish and

embarked upon offering sanctuary to Salvadoran refugees. At the time we didn't know if we were going to get arrested or what. That was a . . . powerful experience—the parish reflecting on what it is to be church. Again the process of talking and dealing with differences, with some African American parishioners saying "the underground railroad helped us, so now it's our time to help them" and others feeling like "yeah but. . . ." I remember thinking in the middle of all that, "no matter what we decide, we are going to be more of a church because we really dealt with . . . how often churches are dealing with other stuff that's not what it's about to be church." According to Linda, they "became the first sanctuary for the Central American refugees in Texas in '83, and they lived with us there."

MINISTRY

For many years the Sisters of St. Mary were teachers with a few nurses. One of the changes that came in this period was an explosion of ministries. Many sisters were, and still are, involved in education in Catholic schools, but others are working in parishes and in the diocese. They have been directors of religious education and liturgists, which are rather traditional roles, but they have also directed priestly formation as director of seminarians (Sister Donna Ferguson), directed children's catechesis for the Fort Worth diocese (Sister Yolanda), and educated Spanish-speaking lay people through what was then called diocesan ministries (Sisters Dorothy and Gabriella). Other sisters offered spiritual direction and retreats, opened bookstores, worked with gangs and people in jails and prisons, and wrote and taught music. The creativity of the sisters is unbounded, and they bring the same energy and solidarity with the poor to these ministries that they brought to everything else that they have done.

Some of these ministries have gained recognition statewide and even internationally. Sister Mary Patricia told me about a wonderful ministry started by Sister Kathy Foster called Casa de

Esperanza de los Niños (House of Hope), which provides a safe place for children in crisis due to abuse, neglect, or the effects of HIV/AIDS. This was during the time when so little was known about AIDS and people were very frightened of it. The sisters of this province decided that the home could be under their auspices, which is one of the reasons that it was able to continue.

Sister Mary Patricia said,

> We took care of the children and learned all sorts of things. One of the stories I love to tell about me is that I came up here for a meeting once and I said there are two things I'll never do. One of them is to live with children and the other one is to eat with children. So I went back home and Kathy said, "What would you think if you moved up here and had the children downstairs?" So I began to eat with children. Occasionally I would have to get up and leave and go into my room and read my detective story for about a half an hour and then come back.

She said, "The first thing we learned is that children are children. They are not children with AIDS—they're children. The first one we had was a child who had been burned over 80 to 90 percent of her body. . . . Somebody was adopting all the children in that family except they wouldn't adopt her because she had AIDS. So Kathy adopted her, and then she adopted a few more, so she has five now." I was told by another sister that Kathy left religious life to raise these children. Another sister said that only one of the five children has AIDS and the oldest one is going to community college with ambitions of becoming a nurse. In 2006 Kathy Foster was inducted into the Texas Hall of Fame for her work on behalf of children.

Sister Josephine is the sister who designed the retreat that helped the community and former sisters to come back together.[8] The web site for "Beginning Experience," her ministry for separated, divorced and widowed people, states,

---

8. To read more about Sister Josephine, see her book, *Letting Go: The Way into Abundance*.

In 1973, Sister Josephine Stewart, a family counselor at the Catholic Renewal Center in Fort Worth, Texas, and a divorced friend, Jo Lamia, attended a Marriage Encounter weekend with the intention of developing a program for engaged couples. In the course of the weekend, Ms. Lamia adapted the Marriage Encounter process to face issues and concerns in her own life that had never been addressed. At the close of the weekend, Sister Josephine saw a profound change occur in her friend.

Sister Josephine and other professionals in grief resolution, counseling, psychology, education and spiritual renewal, adapted Ms. Lamia's writings to outline the process for the Beginning Experience weekend. The copyrighted program was soon in motion throughout the United States, Canada, Australia, New Zealand, Singapore, Great Britain and Ireland. Today, 117 certified teams of peer ministers present the program in communities on three continents.

The Sisters of St. Mary of Namur, like most congregations of religious in the United States, have emerged from the late 1900s as a smaller community, but their charism is as rich and vibrant as ever. In some ways, the exodus of the young sisters led to an opening up of what it means to live the charism of the SSMN and opened the door for a variety of relationships as they move into an unknown future. They do this with the same faith that led the Belgian SSMNs to come to the United States, feeliing called to answer a need and trusting that they would have the means to do so.

Chapter 5

Radical Openness to the Future

EILEEN MARKEY said, "While laypeople looking at the dwindling numbers of aging nuns might ask, 'Can communities of American women religious survive?' the nuns are asking a different question: 'Can the sisters save the American Church?'"[1] Markey said,

> That was the spirit behind the address Benedictine Sister Joan Chittister delivered at the annual meeting of the Leadership Conference of Women Religious in August 2006. She challenged the assembled leaders, who represent 95 percent of American sisters, to embrace the dream envisioned by Vatican II: a renewed church dedicated to God, not tradition. Chittister reminded the assembly of their role as leaven for the world—to be like active yeast causing dough to rise, making it alive. The sisters' mission, Chittister said, is to inspire the rest of the church to reach that promised land, "to be leaven, rather than simply a labor force."

To that end, Markey said, "Sisters in religious congregations across the country are thinking with radical openness about the shape their communities will take in the future. Their ideas are as varied as the congregations, but each is informed by deep confidence in the prophetic role of women religious." The Sisters of St. Mary of Namur in this province demonstrated a kind of radical openness to a different kind of future, beginning, as noted in the last

1. Markey, "Transformation."

chapter, with the reintegration of the former sisters into a new kind of relationship that allowed them to live the charism of the SSMN.

ASSOCIATES

Some of the former sisters were content to have a social relationship and many of them still attend events and in many ways live the charism in their personal and professional life. Other former sisters wanted a more defined relationship. Clarice Peninger is one of the sisters who left the congregation before the major exodus and, like so many others, left without really leaving. She said, "I just couldn't live in community. I continued to believe, though that community had to be about more than living with each other. She added, "I remember thinking at various times—sometimes at recreation, sometimes at prayers . . . how could you ever leave this? And then I did." After she left, she lived with her sister and took classes for a semester at St. Thomas in Houston. She said, "I cried the whole time. I cried and I cried and I cried. . . . I felt like I'd kicked God in the face." She said that she was probably having some kind of breakdown. She said that Mother Devota suggested that she "get out of Dodge."

Clarice had studied to be a teacher and, although she had not yet graduated, she had enough hours that she could teach in one of the sisters' schools in California. She said that two of the sisters she had known in Texas, Sister Francesca and Sister Gertrude, were there. She said, "They just saved my life. They were so good to me." After teaching in California, she came back to Texas, finished her degree at UD, and began to seek a position as a teacher. She said, "Of course, I was going to teach with the Sisters of St. Mary." She said that "Sister Eleanor, who was provincial at the time, finally called me and said that I had left them and that I wasn't going to teach with them, that they'd never hire me. I was stunned. I just couldn't believe it and I was hurt." She taught at some other Catholic schools, finally including a SSMN school, St. Cecilia, and then became principal of Holy Name Catholic School. She remained there until it was closed eight years later, and then became principal of St. Andrew's Catholic School until she retired.

Her first year at St. Andrew's, she said, was the year the sisters "decided to have a gathering of all these people that were attached to them somehow." It was at that gathering that three of the attendees decided that they had a different idea about what they wanted than the rest of the people in attendance. Clarice said, "We wanted something with defined edges. We wanted to be really counted in as part of Sisters of St. Mary. The other ten or so other people were content with just helping out and coming in and out and being friends, but we wanted something more like a form of religious life."

She said that the three of them met again with a few others over Christmas break and began to define a form of membership that took over the title of "associates." This had been a group that had no real definition before but included both a laywoman and a former sister. She said, "In the meantime, Sister St. John and Sister Cecile had both gotten interested in this. Between Christmas and New Year's they had brought in some people who had been novices and Chris, who had been professed and also wanted something like that."

The largest group of associates was begun by Sister Ginny and Sister Patricia Ste. Marie in Wichita Falls, Texas. Ann Smith was one of the first of these associates. Ann is a retired air force nurse and professor who created and directs one of the first nurse residency programs in the country. She had been separated from the church for fifteen years when she met an "a great Irish priest" who asked her why she left the church. She said, "I know exactly why I left. God blessed me with an intellect. I have a lot of questions, and it's clearly not okay to ask [them]. So I'll not return until all of me, including my intellect with its questions, can return with me. And he said, "Ask away!" Ann said that they met monthly for two years and "tore everything apart and put it back together again in a way that I could embrace." She added, "Shortly thereafter, I met

Ginny and Pat [Sister Ginny and Sister Patricia] at Queen of Peace. You cannot be with Ginny for more than about two minutes until you're in . . . stitches. Patricia is incredibly energetic, and she asked if I would help with the RCIA process as a sponsor. Then I'm the one that's laughing."

Ann became aware that the infirmary at the motherhouse had only one nurse left in the province, Sister Mary Elaine. She'd been working at the infirmary without a break, and one of Ann's colleagues at the university who belonged to Queen of Peace said that if she and Ann would work in the infirmary for a week, this would allow Sister Mary Elaine to go on vacation or retreat. Ann said it was quite a change for her, a pediatric nurse, to be working in geriatrics, but that's what they did one summer and have continued to do it ever since.

Ann said that Sister Ginny and Sister Patricia Ste. Marie personally invited about forty women to become associates. She said they told her, "We're thinking about getting together with some of the women who work with us and doing an associate group. We had no idea what that meant at the time. We came to that first gathering and met monthly for years." She said that they shared dinner and prayer and that all of them were involved in ministry with the sisters in some way. She said, "We read a book on simplicity together and talked about it chapter by chapter. We did different scripture studies together." She added that most of the original forty women are still associates, and the number is now close to eighty. They only get together about once a quarter now.

Ann said that they created a skit for the tenth anniversary of the associates. She said they performed the skit and "the last part of it was a slide presentation that was slides of all of the different things that we had done together, the scripture studies, the meetings, the retreats, the parties—everything—because all of us are involved in some aspect of ministry with these women."

Radical Openness to the Future

Because of her medical training, Ann was able to be of assistance to Sister Rosemary in Brazil, where she stayed for a month. She said,

> They had an election while I was down there and the mayor changed. It was a different party. If you didn't vote for him, you lost your job. There was a sister who had set up an immunization program for an entire community, and that program was cut. The day after the election the program was gone, her job was gone and all the immunizations for the kids were gone. I was nuts! At the end of the month I'm thinking "You know every one of these women, they're brilliant first of all. They all speak at least two languages and, in some instances, four. There aren't any of them who are delusional. They all fully recognize the size of the problems that they are up against, but they put one foot in front of the other every day, and they deal with one little problem or issue or person . . . at a time. They do it with incredible joy and very simply." Living with them was just a tremendous experience.

Ann took the tape of the skit about the associates to Brazil with her. She said that one of the sisters

> wasn't quite sure what to make of these women who weren't quite sisters. We had the screen up there and this sister was sitting at the far end, catty-corner from me. Everything on the tape was in English, so Rosemary was translating. There were non-verbal exchanges between Rosemary and me because . . . of . . . shared memories from the slides. At the end of the presentation, this sister, who wasn't sure about the associates, looked at me, and in Portuguese she said (Rosemary translated it for me), "This relationship between the sisters and the associates is a special one, isn't it?" This was from the woman who was the least receptive. And I looked at Rosemary and I said, "It is a very special one," and she translated for her.

There are a number of associates in Fort Worth and Wichita Falls, searching for a way to deepen their life with God, who have been drawn to the Sisters of St. Mary. Most of them have a long history with the sisters, sometimes going back to elementary school. Some of the associates are former sisters; some, like Ann, considered consecrated life and decided it was not their path; others have not considered consecrated life but have been drawn to a deeper life in their current circumstances. Associates make promises, first for a year and then for three years. They promise, "Called by the Spirit to live my baptismal commitment in the spirit of the Sisters of St. Mary of Namur, I choose to live the charism of the Sisters of St. Mary by deepening personal and communal prayer, participating in associate and congregational prayer, striving to live the spirit of the gospel of Jesus, and extending that spirit into service of God's people. With Mary I offer myself with a simple and joyful heart."

OBLATES

After a time it became clear that two of the associates, Diane and Clarice, wanted to create a different kind of religious life. They evolved yet another form of relationship with SSMN, a relationship that they call "oblates." Clarice described the evolution of this form of religious life. She said, "I believed that I was called to a different kind of religious life, but within the Sisters of St. Mary." She also wanted to "make a permanent, perpetual commitment." She said that the provincial

> was unsure about this and kicked it to the general council. They asked me to meet with Sister Marie Julianne, the superior general, when she came to visit Texas and to write down a description of what I wanted. We met, and I explained to her what I was asking to do and gave her my paper. I explained that I realized that "promises" were not canonical, but that I would like to make perpetual promises of *simplicity of lifestyle*, which corresponded to poverty, and I would be financially responsible for myself but would continue to give a portion of my salary to the congregation. *Chastity* (celibacy) would be the same as the vowed sisters. In practicality, today when the congregation asks a sister to undertake a ministry, she discusses it with the provincial council, and they arrive at a decision together. Rarely are they bound to do something under

obedience. I said that my promise would be for *availability*. The sisters could ask me to take on a ministry or project, and we would dialogue about it. If I could, I would comply.

Clarice made a few changes, in response to the sisters' requests, but she said, "I was adamant about one thing. They had written that the promises would be for the western province. I insisted that I was committing to the whole congregation. They eventually accepted this. First, however, they sent Sister Mary Merdian, who was on the general council, to talk with me. She asked what I'd do if they didn't accept my proposal. I said I'd wait for another general council. I think that sealed it."

The name "oblates" was chosen after they reviewed what other congregations were doing. She said that the Benedictines had oblates and, although it wasn't exactly the same as what the SSMN were considering, it "was close." Clarice said, "We had looked for a bit at what exists formally in the church as 'consecrated virgins,' but they are promised to the bishop and are canonical. Sister Marie Julianne had said we probably ought to avoid getting entangled with being canonical. Besides, every time anyone said 'consecrated virgin,' I giggled. It just sounds odd."

Clarice was the only oblate for a while, although she said, "Sister Joan called Diane Annotti an 'oblate in waiting.'" Then Ann Smith became an oblate and "then there was another, and another, and another—we are six in all now. We are a varied group: a divorced mother, a former vowed sister who is now a widow, a single woman, Ann and I, and finally Diane. There are also now three women who have made final promises as oblates in Canada." Clarice added, "Only Ann and I have made final promises at this point. We all believe, though, that we are a new form of religious life. When I explained all of this to the sisters, Sister Devota said to me, 'I'm so glad! I've prayed for you for so long—you are one of those who couldn't live *in* and can't live *out*.' I'm finally home."

Ann said, "Clearly religious life is changing. If you look historically at religious life, it has always been a fruit of whatever the needs of the time, the society, the culture were. And I think that this oblate experiment, if you will, is a part of that. I think it's a fruit of the change in religious life as we have known it for several hundred years now. Whether it will be the change or it's a step along the way, who knows! But it's very exciting for me personally to be a part of that." The oblates wear a medal with an inscription in Latin of the motto of the SSMN: "In simplicity of heart we joyfully offer all to God."

TRANSFER SISTERS

Some sisters are finding a better fit with the SSMN than the communities they entered initially. These sisters represent yet another way of becoming a Sister of Saint Mary. Sister Yolanda was one of the first transfer sisters. She made her final vows with the SSMN on August 14, 2005.

The first thing that Sister Yolanda wanted me to know is that her parents are "both Puerto Rican and migrated to the States." She said, "We were a very Catholic family. Puerto Rico tended back then mainly to be a Catholic small island. We prayed the rosary as a family every night together and went to Mass together and our parents really struggled to send us to Catholic schools. That all kind of nurtured my faith. I'm really blessed with a family who walked with us, and still does."

Sister Yolanda described the night of her First Holy Communion: "That was the biggest day of my life. When one of the school sisters—I think it was in fifth or sixth grade—asked us to write an essay . . . 'What's your vocation? What do you want to be when you grow up?' that was the first time I actually told anybody. I was about eleven or twelve years old, and then it was out—I had said it. I felt . . . , "yes, I think this is it, but I don't want to be a schoolteacher."

Sister Yolanda was close to her brother. "I wanted to socialize and be with him but I knew what I was going to do with my life. I wasn't going to be married. I was to be a sister. She continued,

Radical Openness to the Future

> I met this congregation that was in the parish where I was in New Jersey. Their main missionary catechism (the Sacred Hearts) was parish work. I helped them. I was a catechist since I was going to a Catholic school. They had me teach first grade and kindergarten catechism. I met their founder (because it's a relatively young congregation) who had come to visit them, and I remember when I met her. I think I was in the eighth grade then, and I said to her, "I want to join your congregation. I want to become a sister." She said, "Oh, yes, that's wonderful. You need to pray a lot, but you can't come with us now. Not right now, but you need to pray and stay in contact with the sisters and get a spiritual director." It was great for me to talk about it, and I went back home and told my parents.

She spoke with a priest and he guided her reading. When she finished high school, she entered. She said,

> I was seventeen when I graduated from high school and I was convinced. I said "This is it. This is what I'm going to do." But my dad didn't know how serious I was. When I started processing everything, he said, "I don't think I want you to do this," and he wouldn't sign for me (I was a minor) to get my visa so that I could go to Mexico (because the congregation was in Mexico). He wouldn't sign. We had everything ready. I had my clothing, my suitcases. I was going to travel back with the sisters who were in the parish so I wouldn't fly by myself. You think at that stage that the whole world just crumbles. So everybody left, and I had my suitcases still there. I never unpacked them because they had nun clothes in them.
>
> Every day I would go to my dad and ask. Every day I would go, and there would be my father in tears. "No, no, look at this young man who is after you; look at this other young man. Look, you could go to school. Look at congregations here in the United States," he even would say. "Don't go to Mexico!" But he finally broke down and signed. So quickly I went to get the visa and put everything back in motion and got plane tickets. The night before I left, I went to both him and my mom to get their blessing. Blessings are big in our culture—to have your parents' blessing to do something. He said, "No, that is something I will not give you. You know you are going against my will." I said, "Oh, no! Here I am, this close again.... What

am I going to do?" We went to bed that night, and I was just in prayer the whole night long, asking "What am I going to do?" First thing in the morning when I got up, he was gone. I had made myself a pact. I had prayed and I said, "God, I need to go see my dad at work and ask for his blessing, and if he doesn't give me his blessing, it's fine. Then it is me. I am the one that is trying to do this, and I need to hold off."

I talked myself into that and told my brother, who was going to take me to the airport. My mom was staying home with my sisters, who were younger. I was so crushed! We got to the place where he works, and I just approached him. I think he saw me coming and didn't know what to do. We were both sobbing at this point, and for me it was the deciding factor. But he gave me his blessing, and he helped me get up and just embraced me so firmly. To me that was God's affirmation of my vocation. My dad just said, "Thank you for coming." To me, that was just God's presence throughout.

It wasn't until I got on the plane all by myself that I said, "What am I doing?" I cried all the way to Mexico. Oh, my gosh! There I was, going to another country, and I had never set foot out of the United States. I left my parents, and with God's help I got to Mexico without the slightest clue of what I was going to do, and my Spanish was so-so but not the best. A group of sisters came to pick me up and I finally got through all that stuff. It was culturally an adjustment. That was the beginning of my vocation with that congregation. I was with them for ten years. I did some mission work in Mexico, and then I came to Texas.

Sister Yolanda made vows with this congregation and was happy. They, like so many communities, suffered a lot of turmoil and conflict following the renewal of religious life in the period of Vatican II. Sister felt that she was not able to be and do what she should there, so she left the community. She returned to New Jersey and finished her degree, graduating in social work. Like so many of the Sisters of St. Mary who left in those times, Sister Yolanda found that she had left without leaving. She worked as a social worker and, as she said, "was able to integrate church ministry with the social work with battered women, the shelters, the child abuse, and neglect. It was a different kind of ministry."

She said,

> There was still a void in me because I just knew. I connected the families with churches and with the sisters where I used to be. They started opening up, saying, "How are you doing?" I would go to them. . . . I had to; These families are in your parish, and they need help, and they need clothes, and they need this, and kids need to go to catechism, and you can't charge them . . . you know . . . just get them connected and linked. Then they started saying, "Why haven't you gotten married?" I said, "I have a commitment to God, and that's a lifetime commitment, and I'm doing the work for God. What I do is all for God. I feel the void of not being a religious because I feel I was called for that and I left." So the sisters said, "Have you thought of coming back?" Immediately I said, "I would love to come back."

She added, "I remember the day I got dispensed from my final vows, because I thought, 'It's in the paper, but I'm not taking what I've given and what You've called me for.' That was always on my mind."

Sister Yolanda entered her congregation again in 1995. After many years, she discovered that the problems and hurdles that she had encountered before were still there. She was assigned to Fort Worth in 1999, where she met Sister Dorothy, a Sister of St. Mary.

> Sister Dorothy was the director of all the directors of religious education (DREs) and she had this huge meeting of all the directors. I had gotten there late because they weren't sure where they were going to send me for my last year of vowed time. Well, they needed someone to be a DRE. They said "She is bilingual." So I came in and, sure enough, Sister Dorothy was welcoming and wonderful. I thought "Oh, what a great sister." She gave me her card and told me to call at any time. So naturally I was calling and asking, "What do you do to train catechists? What kind of curriculum can I use?" I kept on calling her and going back and forth and coming in for meetings. Every time I came in, someone from the congrega-

tion would come in with me. The local—they still called them local superiors— would come in. I would say "I'm going to go to the diocese and speak with Sister Dorothy because she's got to tell me about resources." "Oh, I'm going to go with you," the superior would say. So I'd come in. Sister Dorothy would see that . . . we always came in twos. She would say "I'll take you out to lunch so we can talk about this." I'd go home and I'd say, "Sister is going to take me out to lunch," and they'd say, "Okay, well, I'm going to go with you too." She later met Sister Donna Ferguson, who was working with the seminarians, and Sister Gabriella, who was in Hispanic ministries. Sister Yolanda said, "So there were three Sisters of St. Mary right there that I thought were great."

When she found out that her congregation was going to deny her request to make final vows again, she was still in Fort Worth, and she said,

That just took all the wind out of me . . . and the strength. It was good that Sister Dorothy was here, and Father Larry Breedlove, who was the pastor at that time, was a sure source of support for me, and so were some of the sisters that I was with locally. . . . It took maybe a week to gather my strength to speak with Sister Dorothy because Father Breedlove said, "I don't know anything about religious life. You need to speak with someone who does." And sure enough, I did come and talk with her. Her first thing was, "Don't worry. Read about us. We would be happy to just welcome you into our congregation, but find out who we are."

She started giving me literature. Literally, I was still with the sisters doing my mission work because I wouldn't finish all the work until July, and I knew that I needed to do something with myself between May and July and not let anyone know in the parish what was going on. It was just the grace of God again . . . just the grace of God. I went on retreat here. I prayed and prayed and prayed, and I know I had all the support. . . . I met with Sister Joan, who was provincial of the sisters then and told her where I was and said to her, "I think I would like to get to know you more and possibly enter with you." She was also very welcoming and just kind of left it like that, and I said to her, "I'm going to be going to Mexico, and I'm going to re-petition and see if they would consider my old vows or whatever . . . but if not," I said to her, "I would like to come in and not . . . [completely] enter. I want to know more about who the Sisters of St. Mary are. I want to know more about the charism. I want to know more about you. She said, "Well, you are welcome to just come and live with us, just come in and live with us." So I did that. . . . with Sister Joan and Sister Dorothy and Sister Mary. I was commuting back and forth there and helping out at the house and really just living with them and talking to them. Sister Dorothy was in that community and knew very much what my journey was.

I decided to go to Belgium during that time to see where we were born and what we were doing. I said, "Lord, I want to come into this with open eyes and not because I need someone to rescue me because it is be a sister. . . . No, I want to know that this is where you want me [by] the hospitality, the loving, generous, simple way of being and making you feel like you belong and all those signs . . . multiple signs . . . left and right. I had a strong devotion to the Sacred Heart of Jesus since I was a child. Growing up, I remember this huge (to me it was huge, as a young child —it was, because my mother still has it . . .) picture of the Sacred Heart in the living room or in the dining room. My grandmother, my dad, my uncles always had a devotion, and then the congregation I entered was the Sacred Hearts of Jesus and Mary. I said, "I got Mary, but where's Jesus?" Well, our founder or cofounder, Mother Claire, had a great devotion to the Sacred Heart of Jesus, and in our constitution she writes that . . . her spirit and dynamism . . . she drew from the heart of Jesus. It's just in different parts of her life, and I'm saying, "Yes, here's another very real and vibrant connection." It's a link for me where the spirituality of us really draws straight from the heart of God, straight from what energizes me, too, and fills me with life.

Sister Yolanda said that she just kept seeing ways that she fit with the SSMN—the ministry, their way of treating each other with such respect and love and courage. She continued,

> I started hearing about all of their stories when I went to Belgium—how they all started and how they would build houses by the railways and by the rivers. I just thought "Oh,

my goodness!" I just knew more and more that it was a great fit! "This is wonderful!" What pioneering women, what stamina, and what courage! And what they're doing now here in the States, with the Hispanic culture coming in and all the different kinds of cultures, and they are always looking out for the underdog, for the poorest of the poor and the most needy. . . . I just felt, "This is it. This is where I have to be and how God saw . . . saw ahead . . . and just brought me to Fort Worth this last year when I was just going to get knocked off my feet again." That just put the confirmation that this is not a by-chance thing. It is a way of God saying "This is the route you are called to." I have been given that opportunity—the gratitude of my heart I cannot begin to express. There wasn't a moment when God has not been present . . . not one moment in my life. Even in the darkest [time], when I thought "My God, this is not happening" . . . how God has just been there with me, showing me the direction. This whole journey with the Sisters of St. Mary—now I've been with them for five years—to me it's just a continuation of what started when I was seventeen, and it's just so real now.

With the Sisters of St. Mary, I am who I am, and I am loved, respected, welcomed, accepted, encouraged, and I think that's the difference. Where I was, I knew there was a certain way that I needed to be. . . . I felt I was doing my darndest to live within those parameters, but it still wasn't good enough, so . . . there's not the sense of freedom. I could not experience that there with the sisters. . . . You are who you are, and that's who you were welcomed as. They (the Sisters of St. Mary) met me where I was.

The time that I've had with the Sisters of St. Mary has been precious, a treasure. . . . I had the opportunity to go back to Belgium as part of the canonical novitiate year. I was there for six months, and then I did three months in Brazil. I met a whole new province, a whole new different reality . . . the Belgian Province too has a totally different reality than us here in Texas. That gave me our international perspective and also that thread of simplicity and hospitality and joy, and you could just sense that. I sensed it in Belgium very vividly and in Brazil, which was our youngest province, and of course here. I felt like I had such an enormous sense of understanding and knowing what I was coming into . . . welcomed everywhere

I had been.... I owe so much to God and the Sisters of St. Mary for that experience and for being here today and for making my final vows. That day! I had been waiting for that and, again, I did it quickly. Some of the sisters say, "You really did everything fast." Not really —it was a whole lifetime! But it is kind of hard for them to understand that, and I know that.

Sister Yolanda was amazed that the Sisters of St. Mary of Namur encouraged her to keep in contact with her friends from the other congregation. She thought, "This whole part of my life just needs to get cut, severed, and buried. Put a flower on there and don't go back—but that's not it. There are people there who have suffered through this with me and are happy to see me where I am now."

The superior who is there now is such a friend. She came for Sister Yolanda's final vows and the sisters had her sit right behind them in the church. Sister Yolanda said, "That's the hospitality and that's the charism and the spirit, and that has been healing for me. ... It's all about God and that's what really matters. I have their support and their joy."

Other sisters have transferred and, since most of them speak Spanish, they have literally brought a new voice to the sisters, or strengthened the voice that was there in just a few sisters. As Sister Louise said,

> Since we have seen three relatively young Spanish-speaking women asking to transfer to our community, I wouldn't be surprised at anything that happens. I have a feeling that the Lord's just kind of chuckling, saying, "You haven't seen anything yet." Several sisters have mentioned that Sister Mary Margaret had said at some time or another, "We need people to enter, but we need people to enter who are already fully trained." May the Lord continue and may they all have the grace of perseverance in the community. And like someone was saying not too long ago, "We know that they are having occasion to change from one community to another, but we need to change too to be ready to welcome them in whatever state they're coming to us. We need to put our arms around them and say, 'Welcome.

If you need us, we're here. If you need a shoulder to cry on sometime, if you get homesick, we understand.'"

Sister Louise commented that there is a difference between those sisters who enter at seventeen and eighteen and have gone to school with the sisters and knew them and those transfer sisters who are grown women and mature religious but who do not know most of the sisters and may not feel as comfortable asking for help as a younger person. She added, "I think, in a sense, we have to pray to be like Sister Mary Patricia, to have principles but on the other hand to be open and listening to what others have to say to us."

CANDIDATES AND PRECANDIDATES

There are several young women who have entered as candidates or precandidates. They are in various stages of their lives and of their life with the Sisters of St. Mary. One precandidate is in medical school and will not enter until she finishes her schooling and pays off her debts. She participates with the other precandidates when she can. There are some precandidates of nontraditional age and some who are not yet United States citizens. The variety and energy and youth is exhilarating to the sisters.

One of the women who is furthest along in her formation is Lola. While she is on a more traditional path to vowed religious life, her background is far from typical. Lola grew up on one of the islands of the Kingdom of Tonga, "an archipelago of 176 islands (52 of which are inhabited), scattered over 700,000 square kilometers of ocean."[2] According to its official website, the Kingdom of Tonga is "located to the west of the International Dateline . . . the first Pacific nation to greet the new day." Lola's father had moved to the United States and left Lola to grow up with her grandparents. She said one of her earliest memories was when she was a child and her grandparents woke her each morning at five o'clock so that they could dress and walk the twenty-five minutes to church. They

---

2. "Kingdom of Tonga: South Pacific."

did this until her grandfather died, and then Lola and her grandmother continued the practice until she graduated from high school. She said that on their way to church they passed a convent and a large statue of Jesus. She said, "Grandma always taught me, before you pass, you stop and bow your head and say a prayer." She said she did this any time she passed, no matter where she was going . . . and no matter where she was going, she passed that statue. She said that after she reached eleven or twelve years of age, when she passed the statue, she asked Jesus for help and protection. She credits that prayer with the fact that she was not afraid, even walking alone in the dark, because Jesus was with her.

In high school she went to a retreat for prefects. When she talked with the sisters, they asked her what she was thinking about for her future. She said that was the first time anyone asked. But prior to that people would look at her and say, "Are you going to be a nun?" She said that is what she wanted, but until the sisters asked, she had not told anyone. When she told the sisters that she wanted to be a nun, she said that before she entered, she wanted to see her family because she knew that she had a family and brothers and sisters (in the United States) but she didn't know them. But, she repeated several times, "I want to give my life to God. I want to serve God's people." She said that she prayed to God every day asking that she could meet her family one day, and then she added, "before I become a twenty-one year old young woman."

She met her family when she was twenty years old. She had never heard her family's voices or seen them. In 1998 she came home from school and her aunt said, "Your father is here." He and his mother had gone to the cemetery to visit the grave of his father. When he came back, Lola was at the table doing her homework. She said she hugged him, but she did not feel a connection. He was like a stranger to her. She continued to do her homework, but she felt that he was staring at her. She periodically looked at him, and after a time she felt a connection to him. He came over and she was able to have a conversation with him. He told her about her mother and brother and sister. After a time he asked what she would like to do, and she told him she wanted to move to "the big island" where they have a teacher training college because she wanted to teach, but she knew they didn't have the money to send her because only her aunt was working to support them.

He asked if she wanted to go back with him, and she was torn. She said one part of her heart really wanted to, but the other part couldn't imagine leaving her aunts and grandmother, who had been "like moms to me for twenty years. It was hard for me to let them go." Her dad stayed a week and then went back. Lola prayed for strength and courage to talk to her aunts and grandmother. She said her uncles understood because they thought she should be with her mother instead of alone there. It was much harder to talk with her aunts and grandmother. Her dad came back for his younger brother's ordination in 1999, and Lola went to the big island and stayed with her aunt and uncle until her aunt brought her to the United States. Her aunts were "kind of mad," but they accepted it. When she talked with her grandmother the day before she left, it was very difficult. Lola's father said that it had to be Lola's decision. He would not take her; she had to decide to go.

Lola told her dad that she wanted to go with her dad and get to know her family for three years, and then she wanted to enter a convent. Her dad thought she might change her mind, but she did not. She had been in convents on the island, but she wanted to see what convent life was like in the United States. She came in 1999, she worked, and in 2002 she asked her dad to arrange for her to visit some convents. They tried a variety of convents that didn't work out for one reason or another. He talked with Sister Donna Ferguson, SSMN, at the diocesan office, who invited her to come for a visit. She and her father visited with Sister Mary Elaine and Sister Dorothy. She said that they shared their story with her and told her about the Sisters of St. Mary and it sounded good to her. They stayed for Mass and lunch, and then she visited with some of the other sisters. Lola asked to spend a few days with them during

Radical Openness to the Future

her vacation. She said when she asked her boss for time off for a vacation, they asked where she was going, and she said "a convent." They were surprised!

During the visit she had a chance to visit with the sisters, and she said that she felt she opened up. For the first time she shared her story, and she said, "I cried and cried, because I had never shared so much." She was assigned to Sister Francesca as her companion sister. For about three months after that, she came to spend every month for a weekend with the sisters. She said, "I think this is my home," and she became a pre-candidate. She remained in that status for almost two years as she waited for her citizenship papers. Getting those papers was difficult, but she did not give up, even though there were people encouraging her not to continue waiting. Her mother thought she should marry, but Lola was convinced that she wanted to wait as long as necessary because she was clear that this was God's will.

She said that she felt that she had trouble with life but not with her vocation. She discerned that the Sisters of St. Mary was the right place for her, in part because the sisters were dedicated to helping God's people. She read the book for precandidates and then met each week with Sister Francesca to discuss it. Lola said that the book had a lot of good topics, with verses from the Bible and a place to write her reflection about it and a little prayer. It was something to guide her through her precandidacy. She said she "loved those books."

Lola was a postulant, but she couldn't enter until she got her papers. When she got her papers and entered, she said it was a very good day. She lives in a small convent, on the same property as the old motherhouse and the OLV retirement center, with some of the other sisters, including Sister Rosemary. Lola and the other postulant meet weekly with Sister Rosemary to discuss the readings they have done during the week. Sister Rosemary provides different readings each week. Lola works and is attending community college. She is an excellent student and, she said, when she has difficulty with something, she has a large group of teachers and former teachers who help her. She looks forward to becoming a novice and to finishing school so that she can achieve her dream of being a sister and a teacher.

THE FUTURE OF RELIGIOUS LIFE

Ilia Delio commented in an article in *America*, "The new heaven and earth promised by God will not come about by cutting ourselves off from the world or forming Catholic ghettos. It will not unfold through the triumph of ecclesiastical power. It will come about as we follow the footprints of the crucified one, descending into the darkness of humanity and rising in the power of love. This is the path to a new creation symbolized by Christ."[3]

I asked Sister St. John what she sees as the future of religious life. She told a story from the days when she taught religion in an elementary school. She said, "We were talking about religious life and vocations and I said to the kids, 'Do we need religious?' They said, 'Yeah, for schools and hospitals and stuff like that.'" Sister asked them if they had had any lay teachers, and they named the ones that had taught them. Then she asked them, "If this school did not have any sisters here when your children are growing up, would you send your children here?" They said, "Yeah, if it is as good a school as it is now." Sister St. John said, "Then I guess we don't need sisters." One of the children said, "There will always be sisters because there will always be people who need to give their lives to God in that way." Sister St. John said, "She had it. It's not about what you do. . . . The things I have done in recent years weren't even available when I entered. . . . Women didn't work in seminaries, and women weren't chaplains, and women didn't run a parish. It's not what you're going to do. It is who you are going to make the central relationship of your life."

---

3. Delio, "Confessions of a Modern Nun."

Radical Openness to the Future

One of Sister St. John's favorite stories is about the founding of the congregation and the "frontier mentality" of the founders. "The first sisters were women religious in Belgium, and they weren't allowed to be women religious in Belgium." They couldn't wear the habit and they couldn't be called sisters. They were called the "pious women of St. Loup" (St. Loup is the parish there were in). She went on,

> There is a house almost at the confluence of two rivers, and just at the promontory above that confluence is a spot that was used as a fortress since the time of Julius Caesar. There were five thousand soldiers quartered there at the time we were founded, and there were breweries and distilleries along the river there. Five thousand soldiers plus breweries and distilleries and poverty does not make for a promising life for a young girl. Just down the block there was a sewing room, started by two unmarried sisters from a prominent family. They had to find work and, since the only skills they had were needlework, they opened a sewing shop and employed some other women there. (At that time, sewing was done by hand.) At the same time, the pastor of a nearby parish was known for the way any time he found somebody idle he evangelized. He would go to the sewing shop and talk to the young women while they sewed. He even preached a retreat there. He got the idea when he saw the poverty and desperation around him that if only he could teach them to sew, they would have a decent way to make a living.
>
> Two of the young women from the sewing shop came to him and told him that they would like to be religious, but it wasn't permitted in Belgium at that time. He sent them away to another religious community for a few months to get some concept of how you do this thing. We have the story, of course, of the night they came together with a pot and a couple of dishes and a couple of chairs and a table and the whole sense of "yes, we want to give our lives to God and, yes, we could teach sewing to those girls so they could earn an honest living." They began in a little house that was one room deep and three stories high. They taught sewing on the first floor, lived on the second floor, and on the third floor was a little statue of the infant of Prague on a board across the corner. That was their

chapel. There were churches within easy walking distance, so they could walk to Mass. We know they had potatoes and apples that first night—baked potatoes and apples—because they grow there and were easy to cook.

There was a brief pause and then Sister St. John leaned forward with an earnest look on her face and said, "What did they think the future was? Any time I get too worried about the future, I think about them. What did they think was going to happen? They couldn't have imagined it."

Bibliography

"Beginning Experience: Renewing the Light of Hope." Online: http://www.beginningexperience.org.

"Cassata Learning Center." Online: http://www.privateschoolreview.com/school_ov/school_id/26611#Editor.

Chittister, Joan. *The Way We Were: A Story of Conversion and Renewal.* Maryknoll, NY: Orbis, 2005.

Delio, Ilia. "Confessions of a Modern Nun: The Vatican Visitation Prompts Reflection on a Religious Divide," *America*, October 12, 2009. Online: http://www.americamagazine.org/content/article.cfm?article_id=12347.

Donovan, Vincent J. *Christianity Rediscovered.* Maryknoll, NY: Orbis, 2003.

"Kingdom of Tonga: South Pacific." Online: http://www.tongaholiday.com/.

Laughlin, Corinna. "The Second Vatican Council." Online: http://www.stjames-cathedral.org/Prayer/vatican2-1.htm.

Markey, Eileen. "Transformation: Vatican II Was Only a Beginning: Radical Changes Await Religious Life in 21st Century," *National Catholic Reporter*, February 23, 2007. Online: http://findarticles.com/p/articles/mi_m1141/is_17_43/ai_n27162001/.

Nieto, Sonia. *Affirming Diversity: The Sociopolitical Context of Multicultural Education.* New York: Allyn and Bacon, 2004.

Rolheiser, Ronald. *The Holy Longing: The Search for a Christian Spirituality.* New York: Doubleday, 1999.

Slattery, Patrick. *Curriculum Development in the Postmodern Era.* 2nd ed. New York: Routlege, 2006.

Stewart, Sister Josephine. *Letting Go: The Way into Abundance: The Personal Story of the Founder of the Beginning Experience.* N.p.:n.p., 2009. Available the Catholic Renewal Center, Fort Worth, Texas.

Tobin, Mary Luke, SL. "Women in the Church: Vatican II and After." *Ecumenical Review* 37 (1985) 295–305.

www.ingramcontent.com/pod-product-compliance
Lightning Source LLC
Chambersburg PA
CBHW071447160426
43195CB00013B/2046